Modal Expressions in English

Open Linguistics Series

The Open Linguistics series, to which this book makes an impressive contribution, is 'open' in two senses. First, it provides an open forum for works associated with any school of linguistics or with none. Linguistics is emerging from a period in which many (but never all) of the most lively minds in the subject seemed to assume that transformational generative grammar—or at least something fairly closely derived from it—would provide the main theoretical framework for linguistics for the forseeable future. In Kuhn's terms, linguistics appeared to some to have reached the 'paradigm' stage. Reality today is very different. More and more scholars are examining approaches to language that were formerly scorned for not accepting as central the particular set of concerns highlighted in the Chomskian approach, such as Halliday's systemic theory, Lamb's stratificational model and Pike's tagmemics, while others are developing new or partly new theories. The series is open to all approaches, then—including work in the generativist–formalist tradition.

The second sense in which the series is 'open' is that it encourages works that open out 'core' linguistics in various ways: to encompass discourse and the description of natural texts; to explore the relationships between linguistics and its neighbouring disciplines such as psychology, sociology, philosophy, artificial intelligence, and cultural and literary studies; and to apply it in fields such as education and language pathology.

The present book has the virtue of being 'open' in many of these ways—while being soundly centred in 'core' linguistics.

Open Linguistics Series Editor
Robin P. Fawcett, The Polytechnic of Wales

Modal Expressions in English, Michael R. Perkins
Text and Tagmeme, Kenneth L. Pike and Evelyn G. Pike
The Semiotics of Culture and Language, eds: Robin P. Fawcett, M. A. K. Halliday, S. M. Lamb and A. Makkai

Modal Expressions in English

Michael R. Perkins

 ABLEX Publishing Corporation
Norwood, New Jersey 07648

© Michael R. Perkins 1983

First published in the United States in 1983 by
Ablex Publishing Corporation
355 Chestnut Street, Norwood, New Jersey 07648.

Library of Congress Cataloging in Publication Data

Perkins, Michael R., 1949–
  Modal Expressions in English

  Bibliography: P.
  Includes indexes
    1. English language—modality.   2. English language—
semantics.   3. Modality (linguistics)   I. Title.
PE 1315.M6P47   1983   425   83-11890
ISBN 0-89391-209-3

Printed in Great Britain

Contents

List of Figures

List of Tables

Foreword

To seek to understand modality is to set out on a fascinating voyage of discovery in the human mind. Many past studies have focused more or less exclusively on that small set of items known as the 'modal' verbs': *can, could, shall, should, will, may, might, must* and perhaps *ought* (*to*) and *need*. But this is a book about not just modal verbs but *modal expressions*, in a sense that is interpreted here more widely, perhaps, than ever before, and that is shown to permeate the whole language. It is on the basis of this great breadth of modal meanings that Mick Perkins develops a new and insightful model, which provides a persuasive explication of the whole range of modal expressions.

This study is interdisiplinary in its sources, and it is interdisciplinary in the range of those who will gain from reading it. While it is centred squarely in linguistics, it also draws on and contributes to philosophy and (in Chapters 10 and 11) sociolinguistics and child language studies. But I want to suggest that it is also relevant to one of today's most rapidly advancing fields: artificial intelligence. The model relates *forms* of language first to a 'core' *semantics*—reaffirming as it does so what Bolinger (1977: x) has called the 'old principle that the natural condition of a language is to preserve one form for one meaning and one meaning for one form'—and then in turn it relates these meanings out to our *knowledge* of the circumstances and of certain 'laws' that guide our interpretation of them. Computational models are already significantly affecting work throughout the social sciences, and those of us in linguistics who take the view that the semantic features of a language need to be related, not just to each other and to the level of form, but also outwards to a knowledge of the world, will find in this book essential material for work on the area of meaning known as modality.

A word of warning, however. The proposals set out here, explicit as they are, do not constitute a generative grammar for modality. That is not the author's goal. Indeed, I suspect that, as proposals such as these come to be built into holistic grammars, set within related models of the mind and covering a representative range of meaning-types, it will be found that a considerable amount of further work remains to be done. This is, after all, the way it almost always is in scientific enquiry. The contribution of this book is to provide an immensely valuable quarry of facts and insightful explanations in the area of modality that will stimulate and inform work in this area for years to come—including work in constructing fully explicit grammars. The author's meticulous coverage of the literature, together with the sense of completeness and economy in the analysis proposed, should ensure that the book is regularly used by all scholars, of whatever discipline, who investigate the elusive phenomenon of modality.

The Polytechnic of Wales   Robin P. Fawcett
April 1983

Acknowledgements

My thanks go to Robin Fawcett and Bill O'Donnell for their advice and encouragement; to Manfred Bierwisch, John Ford, Dick Hudson, John Lyons, Frank Palmer, Denis Pollard, Nicola Somerville, Peter Tregidgo, Richard Wakely, and David Young for their perceptive comments; to Mid Glamorgan Education Department for allowing me free access to schools to record the data discussed in Chapter 11; to the headteachers, staff, and pupils at Cefn, Gwauncelyn and Heol-y-Celyn primary schools and at Hawthorn Lower Comprehensive School for their assistance and enthusiasm; to Cambridge University Press for permission to reprint portions of my article 'The core meanings of the English modals' which appeared in the *Journal of Linguistics*, Vol. 18 (1982); to Jenny Coates for lending me the proofs of her book; and to my family.

1 Introduction

There is considerable vitality left in the study of modality, despite
the fact that as a philosophical and linguistic concept it has been the
object of continual scrutiny and reformulation since at least the time
of Aristotle. The quantity of recent works on modality by linguists
and philosophers is evidence of the continuing fascination it still
commands. And yet, paradoxically, in spite of the vastness of the
available literature, it is by no means easy to find out what modality
actually is. The problem is that a number of different disciplines and
sub-disciplines have each approached the notion of modality from
different starting points, and in each case the nature of the goal has
come to be defined in terms of the means of approach, with the
result that not only does the question 'What is modality?' have a
number of different answers, but the question itself must be formulated differently according to the type of answer one expects to
obtain. And yet, by restricting oneself to one type of approach
long enough to be able to obtain some clear idea of what kind of
question it is permissible to ask, one automatically cuts oneself off
from other equally valid lines of enquiry which might have had an
important bearing on the very problems one has become involved
with. In view of this, the ideal solution would be to proceed on
several different fronts at the same time—and this, to some extent,
is the strategy which underlies the present study, although for ease
of access I have tried to keep the major approaches reasonably
separate, and have relied on cross-references to establish important
links and build up the overall picture.

Despite its breadth, the book nevertheless has a central theme to
serve as an anchor—namely, the linguistic expression of modality—
and it is first and foremost a linguistic study. It originally developed,
in fact, as a result of speculations as to the relationship between
modal auxiliary verbs such as MAY and other forms such as POSSIBLE,
POSSIBLY, and POSSIBILITY. The term 'modal' is nearly always
used by linguists to refer to a syntactically defined subset of auxiliary
verbs, of which MAY is one, which are regarded as expressing
modality; and although lexical items such as POSSIBLE, POSSIBLY,
and POSSIBILITY from other syntactically defined categories appear

to express the same type of meaning, they are rarely considered in their own right, but are used almost incidentally as paraphrases which serve to illuminate the meanings of the modal auxiliaries that are the primary focus of interest.

In order to find out how such expressions differ, it was first necessary to discover what exactly they had in common. This involved a consideration of the semantic concept of modality, which represents the interests of linguistically oriented philosophers as well as semantically oriented linguists. It soon became clear, however, that the semantic property shared by the modal auxiliaries and their most commonly recognized paraphrases was also an important feature of the meaning of a wide range of other expressions as well, and in order to account for this, it was necessary to recognize a class of 'modal expressions' on the basis of shared semantic characteristics. It was also clear, furthermore, that certain other linguistic phenomena such as tense and IF-clauses also seemed to share the same semantic characteristics. It was only when such a wide range of expressions and other linguistic devices was submitted to a close scrutiny at the same time that it became clear that there were semantic grounds for isolating the modal auxiliaries from other modal expressions, and that no two modal expressions could be said to have exactly the same meaning. By this stage, it was also apparent that the semantic framework which had now been established could also be used to predict the pragmatic interpretation of modal expressions in certain types of context. In addition, when the same framework was used to interpret certain aspects of child language development, a number of affinities were observed between the semantic nature of certain modal expressions, as defined by the model, and the use of such expressions by children at different stages of linguistic and cognitive development between the ages of 2 and 12 years old. In order, therefore, to arrive at an even partial explanation of the differences between modal auxiliary verbs and a few of their paraphrases, it was ultimately necessary to examine modality from perspectives ranging from that of the philosophy of logic to that of developmental psychology—although the enquiry was, I would re-emphasize, motivated at every stage by linguistic considerations.

Although the layout of the book in some ways reflects the progress between the various stages of enquiry referred to in the preceding paragraph, I have tried to organize the text so that the more general issues are dealt with first, followed by a more detailed analysis of the semantics of modal expressions. This is then supplemented by an assessment of how such an analysis is relevant to pragmatic and developmental perspectives of the expression of modality. In Chapter 2, an account of the fundamental philosophical concept of modality is given in terms of the notion of 'possible worlds', and it is then seen how far such a concept is relevant to the way modality is expressed linguistically. In Chapter 3, a 'core-meaning' analysis of the modal auxiliary verbs is proposed and this is extended in Chapters 4 to 8 to include a wide range of non-auxiliary modal expressions, including quasi-auxiliaries; adjectival, participial, and nominal modal expressions; modal adverbs and lexical verbs; and in Chapter 9 to include tense, IF-clauses, and questions. In Chapter 10, it is shown how modality is related to the pragmatic notion of politeness. Chapter 11 traces the development of the expression of modality up to the age of 12 and includes an analysis of modal expressions in a large corpus of data collected as part of an ongoing study of language development in older children being carried out at the Polytechnic of Wales.[1] The final chapter briefly discusses some of the theoretical implications of the book and suggests one or two directions that future research deriving from it might take.

In view of the numerous linguistic studies of modality and the modals which have been published in the last few years, the reader may find it useful if I briefly spell out how the present account relates to and extends what is currently known.

The most recent major treatment of modality at a semantic/conceptual level is that of Lyons (1977: Ch. 17), which begins with the logical characterization of necessity and possibility and proceeds to make a number of important semantic distinctions such as that betweeen subjective and objective epistemic modality. Although a number of linguistic examples are included, their purpose is to support the semantic distinctions which Lyons sees fit to make, rather than to provide a systematic account of the way modality is expressed in any given language. Of those studies which, in contrast, attempt to relate a systematic description of a set of linguistic forms to a notional or theoretical account of modality, Palmer (1979a) provides the fullest most recent account. He describes his particular perspective as follows:

Modality . . . is a semantic term, and I shall use it in this book to refer to the meaning of the modals. It is not necessary to define precisely what kinds of meaning are involved. We take the formal category as our starting point, and it is sufficient for our purpose that the meanings involved are such as to justify characterising them as 'modality' [pp. 4 f.] .

The account in this book differs from those of Lyons and Palmer in the following principal ways: (a) it provides a far more exhaustive account than that of Lyons of the range of linguistic forms used to express modality in a specific language—such as English; (b) whereas Lyons discusses only alethic, epistemic, and deontic modality, the present book includes in addition accounts of dynamic and boulo-maic modality (see 2.1 for definitions); (c) the range of modal forms examined extends far beyond the formal category of modal auxiliaries which has been the focus of attention for Palmer and so many other linguists; (d) beyond simply providing a taxonomy of a limited selection of modal expressions, which is roughly the aim of Palmer, the present study offers a systematic and theoretically motivated explanation for why so many different modal expressions are neces-sary, and shows that expressions such as MAY and BE POSSIBLE THAT are not merely synonymous 'stylistic' variants; (e) finally, the present account extends the discussion of modality to cover politeness (which is touched on only briefly in Palmer's book) and child language development (which is referred to only briefly by Lyons). There are many other differences, of course, but the above are probably the most prominent ones.

A third type of linguistic approach to modality is the corpus-based approach which eschews notional frameworks and restricts itself to an analysis of a corpus of data. The most comprehensive corpus-based treatment of modal expressions to date is Coates (1983), which differs from the present account firstly in that it is a description of actual language behaviour, whereas my account is to a large extent a description of the underlying system[2] from which such usage ultimately derives (although Chapter 11 of this book does include a corpus study); secondly, Coates restricts her account almost exclusively to the modal auxiliaries. There is little common ground, therefore, although the two accounts are far from incompatible, as will be seen at several points in this book.

In addition to the contributions referred to above, a considerable number of references are made in this book to the work of others. This is inevitable in view of the vastness of the literature. Doing research on modality is very similar to trying to move in an over-crowded room without treading on anyone else's feet. I have tried hard not to tread on too many feet and hope I have acknowledged it when I have been unable to avoid it. It is, after all, through tread-ing on the feet of one's predecessors (and sometimes through stand-ing on their shoulders) that one discovers new doors to open. I trust, nevertheless, that I have managed to cross the crowded room of modality by means of one or two routes not formerly used, and that my feet have come to rest in several previously unoccupied spaces, waiting to be trodden on in their turn.

Notes

1. This same corpus, incidentally, will also be referred to occasionally elsewhere in the book.
2. Cf. Lyons (1977: 26).

2 The Scope of Modality

2.1 The concept of modality

One of the first people to commit to writing his ideas on what is now generally referred to as modality was Aristotle (cf. in particular *De Interpretatione*, Chs. 12–13). Central to his discussion are the notions of necessity, possibility, and impossibility, together with the relations which may be perceived to exist between them, and these provide the basis of modal logic, which today is one of the most actively pursued branches of logic. Here, however, I will leave on one side the formal machinery which is the trademark of twentieth century modal logic, and instead consider for a moment the more mundane types of human attitudes and experience from which abstractions such as 'necessity', 'possibility', and 'impossibility' are ultimately derived. To put it quite simply, it would appear that such notions are conceptually grounded in the fact that human beings often think and behave as though things might be, or might have been, other than they actually are, or were. Such a worldview appears to constitute an essential part of the fabric of our everyday lives: the fact that it is raining, that the car has broken down and that I am late for work does not prevent me from imagining myself arriving at work on time, in accordance with my contractual obligations, in a quietly purring car in brilliant sunshine.

To speak in terms of 'things being otherwise', however, is rather vague. If we are to gain anything from such a conception of modality, it will be necessary to get clear what such 'things' are, what it is that they might have been 'otherwise', and what exactly is meant by 'otherwise'.

One way of introducing a little more clarity into the discussion is to reconstrue the notion of 'things being otherwise' in terms of what is true or real in other 'possible worlds'. The analytical apparatus of possible worlds derives ultimately from Leibniz (cf. Rescher, 1979: 16 f., 49 ff.), and is based on the proposal that a proposition can be said to be true in one particular (real or imagined) world and false in another. If I envisage, for example, a world in which there are no human beings, the proposition 'Human beings do not exist' will be true of that world but false of the actual world at the present moment. One can extend this to say that a proposition which is true in all possible worlds is eternally true. The notion of 'possible world' also subsumes the states of a particular world at different points in time (cf. Prior, 1957); thus while the proposition 'General de Gaulle is dead' is true of the actual world at the present moment, it is false of the 'same' world in 1968.[1]

Broadly speaking, the actual world is itself, of course, just one of an infinite set of possible worlds, and as such, it is not exclusively significant. However, if one is specifically interested, as I am here, in the conceptual, as opposed to the purely logical, dimension of modality, one may take the so-called 'conceptualist' line, which 'construes talk about possible worlds as talk about ways in which we could conceive the world to be different' (Haack, 1978: 191). Thus other possible worlds are seen as particularly noteworthy in so far as they contrast with, or are relative to, the current actual world.

So far, then, we can say that to conceive of something being 'otherwise' is to conceive of its being true or real in some non-actual world, or true or real in some state of the actual world at a point in time other than the present moment.

We must now consider what can be meant by 'something' in such a context, and we may usefully begin by noting a distinction made by Lyons (1977: 442 ff.) between three conceptually different types of entity. Physical objects, i.e. persons, animals, and things which 'under normal conditions . . . are relatively constant as to their perceptual properties' and which 'are located, at any point in time, in what is, psychologically at least, a three-dimensional space' are referred to by Lyons as 'first-order entities'. 'Second-order entities', on the other hand, are 'events, processes, states-of-affairs, etc., which are located in time and which, in English, are said to occur or take place, rather than to exist', and 'third-order entities' are 'such abstract entities as propositions, which are outside space and time' and can be assessed in terms of their truth value.

The term 'modality' is not normally used to refer to the status of first-order entities, although etymologically at least, there is no obvious reason why this should not be so. One could, for example, refer to the 'modality' of a first-order entity in terms of its spatio-temporal coordinates (cf. Latin *modus*: 'measure') which could be seen as representing the 'way' it existed in space and time (cf. Latin *modus*: 'manner'). One possible reason why the term 'modality' does not appear to have been used, at least recently, in this sense is that to conceive of a first-order entity existing in other possible worlds raises the philosophically controversial issue of whether

'individuals' in different possible worlds can count as the same—
i.e. the problem of 'transworld identity'—which is something
of a testing ground for philosophers such as Kripke, Putnam, and
Donnellan who challenge traditional theories of meaning (cf., for
example, Schwartz, 1977, and also Haack, 1978: 191 ff.). In view
of the difficulties involved, therefore, I will follow the accepted
usage of not referring to the status of first-order entities in my
discussion of modality.[2]

Events or states-of-affairs (i.e. second-order entities), both of
which I shall usually refer to as 'events' for the sake of brevity,
and propositions (i.e. third-order entities) are both commonly
included in discussions of modality, although logicians tend to
restrict their attention to propositions alone. Rescher (1968: 24),
for example, defines modality as follows: 'When . . . a proposition is
. . . made subject to some further qualification of such a kind that
the entire resulting complex is itself once again a proposition, then
this qualification is said to represent a *modality* to which the original
proposition is subjected'. Such a restricted view is open to the
objection that what is possible, necessary, etc., is not actually a
proposition but, rather, the event referred to, or expressed, by a
proposition (cf. White, 1975: 168 ff.), and thus that it is second-
order entities, rather than third-order entities, which are subject
to modality. Such an objection is not entirely warranted, however,
since it reduces ultimately to the question of the level of abstraction
at which one wishes to discuss modality—i.e., whether one is primarily concerned with the nature of events in the real world or with
the truth-value of propositions which refer to such events—and
there is clearly a direct relationship between the reality of an event
and the truth of the proposition which refers to it (cf., for example,
Lemmon (1962), Hedenius (1963), and Stampe (1975: 22)). As we
shall see, however, the distinction between second- and third-order
entities is particularly significant when considering the way in which
modality relates to the function of individual utterances (cf. 2.2).

We have now established that the kind of 'thing' which can be seen
as being subject to modality is either an event or a proposition, and
that modality itself can be understood in terms of the possible
worlds in which such entities can be conceived of as being real or
true. It remains to examine in a little more detail the various types
of possible world which constitute the meaning of 'otherwise'.

According to the conceptualist view, possible worlds may be construed in terms of conceptual frameworks or contexts within which
an event or proposition has a certain significance or truth-value.
To put it another way, a given event or proposition may be made

relative to, or may be qualified by, a particular worldview, state of affairs, set of principles, etc. Such frameworks are commonly referred to as 'modalities' and these may be classified on the basis of common conceptual properties. One of the most comprehensive summaries of the conceptual domain of modality is that of Rescher (1968: 24 ff.), who includes the following types:

1 *Alethic modalities*, relating to the notion of truth itself:
   It is necessarily true (or: false) that p
   It is actually true (or: false) that p
   It is possibly true (or: false) that p
2 *Epistemic modalities*, relating to knowledge and belief:
   It is known (or: X knows) that p
   It is believed (or: X believes) that p
   It is accepted (or: supposed, assumed) that p
   It is anticipated (or: expected) that p
3 *Temporal modalities*, relating to time:
   It is sometimes the case that p
   It is mostly the case that p
   It is always the case that p
   It has always been the case that p
   It was yesterday the case that p
4 *Boulomaic modalities*, relating to desire:
   It is hoped (or: X hopes) that p
   It is feared (or: X fears) that p
   It is regretted (or: X regrets) that p
   It is desired (or: X desires) that p
5 *Deontic modalities*, relating to duties:
   It ought to be brought about that p
   It ought to be avoided (or: prevented) that p
   It is forbidden to bring it about that p
   It is permissible to bring it about that p
6 *Evaluative modalities*:
   It is a good thing that p
   It is a perfectly wonderful thing that p
   It is a bad thing that p
7 *Causal modalities*:
   The existing state of affairs will bring it about that p
   The existing state of affairs will prevent (or merely: will impede) its coming about that p
8 *Likelihood modalities*:
   It is likely that p
   It is probable that p

The view I shall take of such modalities in this book is that each represents a particular set of laws or principles to which the truth/ actuality of third-/second-order entities is relativized. To take an example of epistemic modality, if I believe that acupuncture cures acne, it could be said that the proposition 'Acupuncture cures acne' is true *relative to* my set of personal beliefs. It may not be true according to the tenets of western medical science, but that is another matter. Similarly, in the case of deontic modality, if I am summoned to appear in court on account of some misdemeanour, according to British law my appearance cannot but occur. I may choose to flaunt the law and stay at home, but this does not alter the fact that relative to the laws of the country I *must* appear.

Although Rescher includes more different sets of principles than is common, his summary is by no means definitive, since the number of modalities one decides upon is to some extent a matter of different ways of slicing the same cake. It seems to me that three general sets of principles can be adduced to account for the more central modalities: firstly, there are modalities such as Rescher's alethic and epistemic modalities which conform to the rational laws of inference, deduction, etc. They are concerned with the interpretation of the world via the laws of human reason. Epistemic modality in particular has been fairly widely discussed by linguists. The term 'epistemic' derives from *episteme*, the Greek word for knowledge; however, the key concept which underlies modality seems to me to be the state of *lack* of knowledge which has been referred to by linguists in terms of 'non-factivity' (cf. Kiparsky and Kiparsky, 1970). To know (KNOW is a factive predicate) that a proposition is true presupposes that it actually *is* true; whereas, say, to be certain (CERTAIN is a non-factive predicate) that a proposition is true does not presuppose that it is true.[3] It is true, of course, that one can 'know' something and be mistaken, but then one's 'knowledge' is, by implication, no longer knowledge. It must, therefore, be 'knowledge', as opposed to knowledge, which is relevant to a discussion of epistemic modality as it is understood here.

Perhaps because of such problems, many identify epistemic modality instead with the concept of belief.[4] Antinucci and Parisi (1971), for example, incorporate in their discussion of epistemic modal verbs a two-place predicate $BELIEVE_{XY}$, which expresses a relation of belief between a person X and a state of affairs Y. This, in turn, recalls Hintikka's (1962: 10 ff.) epistemic operator $B_a p$, which can be glossed as '*a* believes that p'. Searle (1976: 10) similarly shows belief to be a sincerity condition for 'representatives' which, as we shall see in 2.2, are related to the notion of epistemic modality.

The second general set of principles concerns modalities, such as Rescher's deontic modalities, which are defined in terms of social or institutional laws. These can be of two general kinds: on the one hand are laws which are explicitly laid down by some legal authority or institution and which define a set of rules of behaviour for some specified social group; on the other hand are the usually less formal rules relating to social status, according to which one person may be said to have personal authority over another. There is, however, no absolute dividing line between the two. Boulomaic modalities have certain affinities with deontic modalities, but these will be discussed in the following section (2.2).

The third general set of principles involves what Rescher calls 'causal' modalities, which are concerned with the relationships between empirical circumstances or states of affairs and the states of affairs which are seen as following from them. There are numerous philosophical accounts of causation, which may be roughly divided into those, on the one hand, which follow Hume in arguing that causes and effects are merely similar sets of objects or events which appear to be invariably conjoined, and that the idea of necessary connection between them is merely a result of our continually seeing them thus conjoined; and those, on the other, which argue that there *is* a necessary connection between cause and effect, whether it be defined in terms of purpose, function, volition, or more generally as the set of conditions necessary to bring about a change. Neither of these accounts seems to me entirely appropriate for the description of what Rescher lists as 'causal modalities' which involve a disposition of a set of circumstances towards the occurrence of some event, rather than a necessary relation between cause and effect. To avoid this latter connotation, I shall use instead of 'causal modality' Von Wright's (1951: 28) term 'dynamic modality' (which is also used in a similar sense by Palmer, 1979a) to refer to the relationship which exists between circumstances and unactualized events in accordance with natural laws—e.g. those of physics, chemistry, biology, etc. I shall also treat as subcategories of dynamic modality Rescher's likelihood modalities and boulomaic modalities, since both are also primarily concerned with disposition towards the occurrence of non-actual events, although in the case of boulomaic modalities this disposition derives from a conscious human source, and the laws involved are specifically psychological and arguably a subcategory of natural laws. Lyons (1977: 846) remarks that 'physical necessity and possibility, which, though it is not normally judged to fall within the province of modality, is obviously relatable to, and at times may be indistinguishable from, objective deontic modality'. In this book, however, I shall use the term 'dynamic' to refer to physical necessity and possibility, as noted above, and shall use the term 'deontic' in the apparent sense of Lyons's 'subjective deontic'—i.e., that which is concerned with principles or laws deriving from human agents within a social context.

The three sets of general principles proposed above—namely rational laws (or the laws of reason), social laws (or the laws of society), and natural laws (or the laws of nature)—define three different types of possible world in which the truth/actuality of propositions/events may be assessed, and will form the background against which the precise nature of English modal expressions may be determined.

I have not yet accounted for Rescher's temporal and evaluative modalities. Temporal modality, which has its own particular conceptual domain, will be discussed in its own right in 3.4, 9.2, and elsewhere. Evaluative modality, on the other hand, will be ignored for the purposes of this book, for the following reason: evaluative predicates such as GOOD, AMAZING, WONDERFUL, etc., as used in frames like IT'S . . . THAT p, are very often factive—i.e., like KNOW, they presuppose the truth of the expressed proposition. This tie-up between evaluation and factivity is by no means accidental. It has been argued by Rosenberg (1975), for example, that the fact that certain lexical items may be factive in one context but non-factive in another (as shown by Karttunen (1971)) can be explained by a pragmatic principle of 'emotional reaction'—namely that 'people react emotionally to states and events that exist (rather than to non-existent, fictitious, or hypothetical ones)'. Since the primary function of a factive predicate is to comment on, or evaluate, an aspect of the world that is, rather than of some world that might be or might have been, evaluative modality does not come within the scope of the particular approach to be adopted here.

2.2 Utterance functions and their relationship to modality

So far, we have been concerned with the conceptual status of modality, but since our primary concern will be with the linguistic expression of modality, we must now assess the concept in terms of the way it relates to language use.

There appear to be two basic uses to which language is put: we can use language either to comment on, or assert, our interpretation of the world, or else to effect some change in the world through the mediation of other agents. Thus Austin (1962) distinguishes between 'constative' and 'performative' utterances; Halliday (1973) between the 'ideational' and 'interpersonal' macro-functions of language; and Davies (1979: 15) between 'interpretational meaning', which corresponds to the 'interpretation of the world', and 'inter-actional meaning', which corresponds to 'the establishment and embodiment of social relations and interactions' including 'the manipulation of social reality'. The former of these two basic functions represents an essentially static view of the world, and the latter a dynamic one. The two can be made to appear intertrans-lateable if one argues that a state may be regarded dynamically as an arbitrary point of transition within a process, and that change may be regarded statically as a sequence of discrete states, but both these views are philosophically and mathematically problem-atical in that they raise the question of how we are to define the intervals between discrete entities, whether they be regarded as temporal or spatial (cf., for example, Lucas, 1973), and it seems more plausible to regard this basic functional distinction as a direct reflex of two separate strategies which human beings employ in their attempts to make sense of the world and be part of it. There is evidence of such strategies very early on in children's use of language, certainly well before the age of 18 months, and they have been variously described as 'descriptions' vs. 'request functions' (Antinucci and Parisi, 1973); 'reportative' vs. 'overt performative utterances' (Gruber, 1973), and 'mathetic' vs. 'pragmatic' functions (Halliday, 1973 and 1975).[5]

In addition to this fundamental distinction, a number of finer distinctions can be made. One of the most comprehensive taxonomies of utterance functions to date is that of Searle (1976) whose two major criteria are 'illocutionary point'—i.e. the point or purpose of an utterance—and the 'direction of fit between words and world' —i.e. the way in which the propositional content of an utterance relates to the real world. Of Searle's five major categories of illocu-tionary act—namely 'assertives',[6] 'directives', 'commissives', 'expres-sives', and 'declarations'[7] —directives and commissives 'undertake to shape a future reality to match what is said now; they work to control in language what the speaker will do (commissives) or what the hearer will do (directives)' and declarations similarly attempt to fit world to words, except that they do so 'immediately, not mediately' (Hancher, 1979: 3). It appears, then, that directives, commissives, and declarations are specific varieties of the 'instru-mental' function of language. In contrast, the illocutionary point of assertives is to 'commit the speaker (in varying degrees) . . . to the truth of the expressed proposition' (Searle, 1976: 10)—i.e. the direction of fit is words to world—and that of expressives is to 'express the psychological state specified in the propositional content' (ibid. p. 12). With expressives, there is no direction of fit—'the truth of the expressed proposition is presupposed' (ibid. p. 12). Assertives and expressives, therefore, are specific varieties of the 'representational' function of language.

In this book I will be concerned principally with the general utterance functions which I have called 'instrumental' and 'representational'. However, I shall have little to say about commissives and declarations, and nothing at all to say about expressives, which, like Rescher's evaluative modalities, presuppose the truth of the expressed proposition and are therefore factive. This leaves assertives, on the one hand, which, at least as characterized by Searle, appear to have close affinities with Rescher's epistemic modalities, and directives, on the other, which have close affinities with Rescher's deontic modalities. Despite such affinities, however, it should be noted that Searle's and Rescher's taxonomies are concerned with two entirely different classes of phenomenon—namely illocutionary acts and modal concepts respectively. Whereas it is not always essential to distinguish between second- and third-order entities in a discussion of modality purely as a concept, it is extremely important to make the distinction when discussing the functions of utterances: the instrumental function of language, as exemplified in directives, is specifically concerned with the bringing about of events—i.e. second-order entities; whereas the representational function of language, as exemplified in assertives, is specifically concerned with the assessment of the truth of propositions—i.e. third-order entities.

Rescher's alethic, temporal, causal (i.e. dynamic), and likelihood modalities, unlike his epistemic and deontic modalities, have no clear functional analogue in Searle's system. However, Rescher's boulomaic modalities—i.e. those relating to desires, hopes, fears, etc.—do appear to be related to a particular speech function, although no such category is included in Searle's taxonomy. There seems to be no reason, however, why a further subcategory of 'desiderative' illocutionary acts should not be included, whose function is to express the speaker's hopes, desires, fears, etc. *vis-à-vis* some non-actual state of affairs. Lyons (1977: 826) points out that the 'desiderative and instrumental function[s] of language: that is to say, . . . the use of language, on the one hand, to express or indicate wants and desires and, on the other, to get things done by imposing one's will on other agents' are both closely related to the category of deontic modality in that 'I want the book' will often be interpreted as 'Give me the book'. It is nevertheless clear that, in English at least, there is a clear semantic distinction between expressions such as WANT, DESIRE, HOPE, YEARN FOR, on the one hand, and ORDER, DEMAND, INSIST, OBLIGE, on the other, and therefore boulomaic, as opposed to deontic, modality, and the desiderative, as opposed to the instrumental, function of utterances, will both have a place (albeit a minor one) in this book.

Although little more need be said, for the moment, regarding the characterization of assertives, there are two important subcategories of directive which should be noted. Lyons (1977: 745 ff.) distinguishes between what he calls 'mands' (e.g. commands, requests, and demands)[8] and 'non-mands' (e.g. warnings, recommendations, and exhortations) on the grounds that mands 'are governed by the particular speaker-based felicity-condition that the person issuing the mand must want the proposed course of action to be carried out'. For a directive to be classed as a non-mand, on the other hand, it is sufficient that it be 'governed . . . by the more general addressee-based condition that the speaker must believe that the addressee is able to comply with the directive'.

The representational and instrumental functions of language may be partially distinguished in English by means of the formal differences between the indicative and imperative moods. Thus:

1 The king is dead.
2 It's raining.
3 Time and tide wait for no man.

would typically be uttered to assert the truth of their respective propositions, and:

4 Pass the sugar.
5 Be reasonable.
6 Stop it.

would typically be uttered with the intention of bringing about the event referred to in their propositional content. None of the propositions expressed in (1) to (6) is modalized[9] and thus (1), (2), and (3) may be regarded as 'categorical' assertives or assertions[10] (cf. Lyons, 1977: 745), and (4), (5), and (6) as 'categorical' directives, where 'categorical' refers to the fact that the truth of the propositions expressed in (1), (2), and (3), and the occurrence of the events referred to in (4), (5), and (6), are not *explicitly* dependent upon, qualified by, or relative to, any alethic, epistemic, temporal, deontic, or dynamic conceptual framework.

By adding a modal expression to each of (1) to (6) we get:

1a The king must be dead.
2a Perhaps it's raining.
3a It's conceivable that time and tide wait for no man.
4a You must pass the sugar.
5a I order you to be reasonable.
6a It's necessary for you to stop it.

(1a), (2a), and (3a) would typically be uttered as modalized assertions[11]—i.e., the speaker's commitment to the truth of the proposition expressed in his utterance is qualified. With (4a), (5a), and
(6a), on the other hand, things are not quite so clear. Although
they *could* be uttered as modalized directives[11]—i.e., the speaker's
commitment to the actualization of the state of affairs referred to in
the propositional content of his utterance is qualified—this does
not have to be the case. (4a), (6a), and even (5a) could, in fact,
also be uttered as assertions. Thus a modalized directive appears to
be formally indistinguishable from a modalized assertion. There is a
sense, of course, in which even a categorical assertion can be regarded
as a directive in that it may constitute an attempt to get one's addressee to believe the truth of what one is asserting. This is why Austin
(1962: lecture XI) ultimately came to regard constatives as a special
kind of performative, and why Ross (1970) analyses declarative
sentences as performative sentences with a deleted performative
verb. Halliday (1970b: 143 f.), using a different approach, argues
that clauses simultaneously realize at least three different functions,
and Fawcett (1980) argues for a grammar with as many as eight
functional components.

However, in spite of such apparent functional polysemy, there
does appear to be a way of clarifying the distinction between categorical assertions, modalized assertions, categorical directives, and
modalized directives on partially formal grounds. Firstly, consider
the differences between the following:

7 It's cold in here.
8 Shut the window.
9 Can you shut the window?

There is no doubt that (7) could be used to get someone to shut the
window, and yet there appears to be no formal feature of (7) which
would enable one to predict this. In fact if (7) were uttered by
someone in a submarine, it is extremely unlikely that it would be
regarded as a request to shut a window! It appears, then, that the
use of (7) to issue a request is entirely a pragmatic matter—i.e.,
the information which determines whether or not it is to be understood as a directive is entirely contextual.

With (8), however, there are good grounds for arguing that the mood of the verb is directly related to the directive function which would normally be associated with an utterance of (8). There are certain contexts where this would not be the case (cf., for instance, the examples and references given in Downes (1977: 78)), but these may reasonably be regarded as exceptional cases.

Sentences like (9)[12] seem to be somewhere between sentences like (7) and (8). Although they are not formally directives, as could be argued for (8), they are at the same time different from sentences like (7) in that they are often conventionally used as directives, and (9) could easily be a polite version of (8). The way in which (9) differs from (7) and (8) can be seen in the extent to which each formally realizes the following conditions (proposed by Holmberg 1979: 238) which are necessary if an utterance is to be interpreted as a directive:

a. The action is volitional (that is, the main verb denotes a volitional action).
b. The actor is the addressee (where 'actor' is defined as the individual of which the action is predicated; this is to say, the NP denoting the actor must be such that it can refer to the addressee).
c. Time reference is non-past.

Sentence (7) meets condition (c), but that is all. For (7) to be used as a directive, conditions (a) and (b) must be present in the context of utterance.

Sentences (8) and (9) both meet all three conditions but differ in that whereas (8) would almost invariably be uttered as a directive, (9) is dependent to a much greater extent upon the context of utterance as regards its status as a directive. Nevertheless, (9), although not formally a directive to the same extent as (8), still contains a greater number of formal elements that are compatible with a directive interpretation than (7), and thus (9) and (7) are formally distinguished in this respect. Brown and Levinson (1978: 137-47) argue, in fact, that the formal structure of indirect speech acts like (9) is governed by the demands of universal rational politeness strategies, and is therefore approximately the same in all languages.

Holmberg (1979: 238 f.) refers to sentences like (8) as 'literal directives', to sentences like (9) as 'A-indirectives' ('indirective' is a blend of 'indirect' and 'directive') and to sentences like (7) as 'B-indirectives', and gives the following additional examples of A-indirectives:

10   I'd like you to close the door.
11   I must tell you not to touch that bust.
12   Would you mind waiting outside?
13   Why don't you go away?
14   Are you able to reach my coat and hand it to me?
15   You'll be here tomorrow at 9.30 sharp.

Holmberg's category of A-indirectives is, in fact, equivalent to what I have referred to above as 'modalized directives', and (10)–(15) may be seen as modalized versions of the following literal ('categorical' in my terminology) directives:

10a Close the door.
11a Don't touch that bust.
12a Wait outside.
13a Go away.
14a Reach my coat and hand it to me.
15a Be here tomorrow at 9.30 sharp.

Although there are often affinities between modal categories and utterance function categories, as we have seen above, the two are theoretically distinct. Thus, for example, deontic modality may be present in either an assertion or a directive. Whether a sentence like:

16   You must not tell lies.

is uttered as a command (i.e. = 'I order you not to tell lies') or as an assertion (i.e. = 'Moral honesty requires you not to tell lies'),[13] it remains deontically modal.

In view of this, it will be necessary to take separate note not only of the particular conceptual subcategory of modality which a given expression realizes, but also of the way in which it interacts with the function of the utterances in which it may be used.

Finally, it should be noted that although I shall recognize a number of different conceptual and functional distinctions in my analysis of modal expressions, it will nevertheless be important not to lose sight of the fact that modality itself may be regarded as a single conceptual system which takes on different characteristics according to the various other semantic and pragmatic systems with which it intersects, and this point will surface at various places throughout the book. Modality is essentially the qualification of the categorical and the absolute as realized, for the purposes of this book, within the code of language. Instead of asserting absolutely that such and such is the case, one may—perhaps for reasons of uncertainty, tact, or politeness—indicate that the truth of what one has to say is by no means assured; that it is based merely on conjecture or that it can be verified only at some point in the future. Instead of issuing a categorical directive, one may—perhaps because one's personal authority is inadequate, because one does not want to assume direct responsibility, or again purely out of politeness—indicate that one is acting only in accordance with some set of rules; or that one is not laying an obligation but merely asking for one's personal wishes to be taken into account. And yet, whatever the precise nature of the qualification, it will always be effected by showing the validity of what one is saying to be relative to some conditional framework, which could be anything from one's own conceptual limitations to the Ten Commandments, or indeed, any other similarly circumscribed world.

2.3 Modality and linguistics

The primary concern of linguistics is with linguistic form. Although semantics is clearly of central importance in any study of language, the analytical strategy most often used by linguists is first, to isolate a class of formal items on distributional grounds, and only then to attempt to characterize them semantically. Discussion of modality in linguistics has, therefore, been concerned almost exclusively with the syntactic class of modal auxiliary verbs, or 'modals', which constitutes the only formally coherent class of modal expressions in English. Besides the modal auxiliaries, however, there is a wide range of linguistic devices in English which are equally deserving of the semantic lable 'modal', but in linguistic treatments these are invariably mentioned only in so far as they may serve as paraphrases to illuminate the meaning of the modal auxiliaries. Thus a group of expressions such as MUST, IT'S NECESSARY TO, IT'S OBLIGATORY THAT would be regarded by many linguists as differing little, if at all, in meaning. Kempson (1977: 73 f.), for example, states that the following two sentences:

17 The reports you send in must be as simple as possible.
18 It is obligatory that the reports to be sent in by you be maximally simple.

are semantically equivalent but differ in terms of their stylistic characterization. Lodge (1977: 46) similarly refers to MAY, PERHAPS, IT'S POSSIBLE THAT, and THERE'S A POSSIBILITY as 'a range of stylistic choices'. Some writers do hint that so-called 'stylistic' differences are not necessarily to be dismissed quite so lightly in discussions of semantics. Lyons (1977: 806), for example, feels that IT IS POSSIBLE THAT and THERE'S A POSSIBILITY THAT are 'more appropriate . . . for the expression of objective epistemic modality'[14] than MAY.

However, the relative 'appropriateness' of different modal expressions, even on the rare occasions when it is actually considered, is never dealt with in any detail, and more often it is ignored altogether. It may indeed be the case—and I shall argue later that in fact it is the case—that the way in which modal auxiliary verbs are used to express modality is different in some sense from that in which non-auxiliary modal expressions are used, but the syntactically oriented approach to modality which motivates most linguistic treatments is unable to throw any light on the issue, since it is geared towards emphasizing the similarities between the modals and their paraphrases, rather than their differences.

It is generally the case in any purportedly 'scientific' discipline that what cannot be encompassed within an existing theoretical framework will be ignored, or at most shelved until such a time as a suitable framework should become available, and this is what appears to have happened in the case of modal expressions in linguistics. Because of the syntactic and 'stylistic' heterogeneity of most modal expressions—but in spite of their semantic homogeneity as a class (i.e. they all express some kind of modality)—there has never been any attempt at a systematic classification of modal expressions. It will be one aim of this book to propose such a classification, and not merely of modal expressions but also of other linguistic devices whose major function, it will be argued, is also to express modality.

2.4 Some terminological issues

Up to now a number of general theoretical terms have been used with little or no explanation. Before I can proceed further, however, it will be necessary to give a more precise indication of how these terms are to be understood.

I shall use the term 'semantic' to refer to a linguistic unit to which can be attributed a meaning which is independent of the environment in which the unit occurs. Examples of semantic units are sentences and lexical items. Some examples of linguistic phenomena which are not semantically independent in this sense are lexically empty items such as auxiliary DO and the 'dummy' subject IT, question tags like ISN'T IT and subject-verb inversion. All of these are essentially syntactic phenomena, which is to say that although they may convey meaning, they cannot do so independently of some broader linguistic context. Sentences, of course, although they can be referred to as independent semantic units, are also syntactic in that their internal coherence depends upon their component lexical items conforming to certain organizational principles.

I shall use the term 'expression' to refer to linguistic units whose semantic content cannot be expressed as a complete proposition, as opposed to sentences and clauses whose semantic content can be expressed as (one or more) propositions. The class of expressions will thus include the class of lexical items. Some examples of expressions which are not simply single lexical items are: IT'S EXPECTED THAT, THERE'S A CHANCE OF, UNDER CERTAIN CIRCUMSTANCES, and IN MY OPINION.

The term 'utterance' will be used to refer to a spatio-temporal equivalent, or realization, of a sentence, which is expressed through the medium of speech in some unique event. The context of such an event—i.e. its spatio-temporal coordinates, the attitudes, beliefs, knowledge, etc. of its participants—will be referred to as the 'context of utterance'. I regard the context of utterance as the domain of pragmatics, and will use the adjective 'pragmatic' in this sense. The term 'contextual' will also be used to overlap with 'pragmatic', but in addition will include sentential environment (or 'cotext') when it refers to an expression. For every utterance, it will, in principle, be possible to distinguish a 'formal component'—i.e. a sentence—which can be discussed in terms of its syntax and semantics, and a 'pragmatic component'—i.e. a context of utterance. Any meaning which is realized in the formal component of an utterance can be said to be 'formally explicit', or simply 'explicit'. Thus Holmberg's (1979) 'literal directives', 'A-indirectives', and 'B-indirectives' (cf. 2.2) may be distinguished along a scale of formal explicitness.

Two utterances may, in theory, be equivalent in their overall meaning (i.e. semantic *and* pragmatic meaning), but may at the same time differ as regards the way the meaning is distributed between their formal and pragmatic components. Consider, for example, an utterance X of which the formal component may be expressed as: 'Idiot' and an utterance Y of which the formal component may be expressed as: 'I formally state that you are of that class of persons which is characterized by mental deficiency and/or foolishness'. Assuming that the utterances X and Y are equivalent in their overall meaning, the meaning of X is far less formally explicit, and, one might add, far less formally complex, than that of Y. All the additional information realized in the formal component

of Y must somehow be available in the pragmatic component—
i.e. the context of utterance—of X if X and Y are to be regarded
as equivalent.[15]

The two theoretical extremes of such a scale of formal explicitness would be (a) a case where no information at all were expressed
formally—as in a gesture, for example—but this could no longer
be called an utterance; and (b) a case where no information at all
were expressed pragmatically. This latter contingency could be
regarded as a sentence occurring in a 'null' context[16] (in other
words, the sentence would constitute its own context and would be
equivalent in overall meaning to its utterance) which is, in fact, a
practical impossibility, for, as Searle (1979: Ch. 5) has convincingly
argued, even the literal meaning of a sentence can be understood
only 'against a set of background assumptions about the contexts
in which the sentence could be appropriately uttered'. This does
not, however, invalidate the distinction made here between semantic
and pragmatic meaning. For example, in order to understand the
semantic meaning of a sentence like:

19 The door is open.

we need to know that doors are things which can be opened or
closed (i.e. background contextual assumptions), but this does
not directly bias us towards interpreting the sentence, when
uttered, as a statement, order, threat, etc., which is purely a pragmatic matter.

The distinction between the formal and pragmatic components
of an utterance also makes it possible to distinguish between what
might be called 'primary illocutionary force'—i.e. the illocutionary
force of a sentence independent of its context—and 'secondary
illocutionary force' which is due to the context of utterance. Thus
a sentence like:

20 You can go now.

when uttered as a directive can be regarded as having the primary
illocutionary force of an assertion and the secondary illocutionary
force of a directive. It can be taken as a general rule that if there is
ever any conflict between primary and secondary illocutionary force,
the latter will always override the former. Hence, the illocutionary
force of an utterance will coincide with that of its formal component (i.e. its primary illocutionary force) only if its secondary
illocutionary force is not such as to prevent it. It is not necessarily
the case, however, that the overall illocutionary force of an utterance
will have to be pragmatically *derived* from its primary illocutionary

force. Certain forms are sometimes conventionally associated with an illocutionary force which is not their primary one (as is the case with indirect speech acts—cf. 2.2 above) and if circumstances are such as to sustain the conventional meaning, the primary illocutionary force need never enter into the picture.

I shall also distinguish between the 'core meaning' of an expression and its contextual meaning, but since there is some disagreement as to how such a distinction should be represented in the case of modal expressions in particular, and even as to whether such a distinction is possible in principle, I shall deal with it in Chapter 3, together with a number of other related issues.

Notes

1. For a more detailed formal account see McCawley (1981).
2. This point receives further discussion in 5.4.2.
3. Cf. White (1975: 80): 'A man can be (or feel) certain that p without knowing that p, still more without knowing that he knows that p, and, indeed, even without being right in supposing that p. One man can be certain that p and another be certain of the opposite, but if someone knows that p, no one can know the opposite. Contrariwise, a man can know that p without being (or feeling) certain that p and without thinking or feeling that p is certain, though not without being right in supposing that p. Indeed he may well know something without either knowing or even thinking that he does know it'.
4. For a more precise discussion of the relationship between the concepts of knowledge and belief, see Alexandrescu (1976), Hintikka (1962), and Ryle (1949: 128 f.).
5. See also the discussion in Griffiths (1979).
6. In Searle's 1976 article, the term 'representative' is used. In a later version, published in Searle (1979), this is replaced by 'assertive' on the grounds that 'any speech act with a propositional content is in some sense a representation' (p. viii).
7. Searle also includes the subcategory of 'assertive declarations', and Hancher (1979) expands Searle's framework to include what he calls 'commissive directives', 'cooperative declarations', and 'cooperative commissives'.
8. There appears to be some disagreement regarding the extent to which it is possible to characterize such functional categories in syntactic and semantic terms. Green (1975: 753), for example, states that demands 'cannot be reported with *tell* or *ask*, but only with *demand*'; whereas Lyons (1977: 753), apparently in flat contradiction, states that 'commands and demands can both be reported by means of the same kind of statement, for example, "I told him to free the prisoner immediately" '.
9. This is not strictly the case with (1), (2), and (3) since, unlike (4), (5), and (6), they have an overt tense marking and could thus be said to be temporally modalized. However, since the so-called present tense is, from the point of view of modality being taken here, the least marked tense form, and since an indicative sentence must always have some tense marking, I will for present purposes regard (1), (2), and (3) as being unmodalized.

10. I will from now on use the term 'assertion' in preference to Searle's 'assertive' in view of the wider currency and applicability of the former.

11. Strictly speaking, it is not the assertion or directive itself which is modalized, but rather the truth of the proposition or the occurrence of the event referred to in the assertion or directive; but I shall nevertheless continue to use terms like 'modalized assertion' and 'modalized directive' as convenient abbreviations. A similar convention is apparently subscribed to in a number of linguistic treatments of modality, where the modality of *sentences* is referred to (cf., for example, Boyd and Thorne (1969), Householder (1971) and Ransom (1977)), although it is, in fact, as Halliday (1970a: 347) puts it, 'the process expressed by the clause' which is modalized.

12. Sentences like (9) have variously been referred to as 'whimperatives' (Sadock, 1970 and elsewhere), 'hedged performatives' (Fraser, 1975), and 'indirect speech acts' (Searle, 1975). Gordon and Lakoff (1971) discuss the same phenomenon in terms of 'conversational postulates', and Katz (1977: 10 ff.) would describe (8) and (9) as having the same propositional content but as differing in their 'propositional type'. All of these accounts would appear to owe a great deal to Grice (1968).

13. Lyons (1977: 828) refers to this type of utterance as a 'deontic statement'.

14. Lyons's distinction between subjective and objective epistemic modality is roughly that in the former case an uncertainty exists in the speaker's own mind about a given state of affairs, whereas in the latter case the unverifiability is due to the nature of the state of affairs itself. For a more detailed account see Lyons (1977: 793 ff.).

15. Katz (1977: 46 n.) points out that Ross (1970) 'seems to have confused the constative/performative distinction with the explicit/implicit distinction' in his performative analysis of sentences. In my terms, what Ross has done, in fact, is construe the pragmatic component of declarative utterances as part of their formal component. For further discussion, see also Chapter 7 below.

16. Cf. Katz's (1977: xiii) characterization of 'theories of pragmatic performance' as 'explications of the principles speakers and hearers employ to work out the contribution that specific contextual information makes to utterance meanings, relative to the overall assumption that the closer a context is to the null context the larger the proportion of sentence meaning in utterance meaning and the less these principles are required to work out'.

3　Modal Auxiliary Verbs [1]

3.1 Introductory

It has already been pointed out (2.3) that most linguistic studies of modal expressions begin and end with an analysis of the modals. Here, however, an analysis of the modals will constitute a first step in a much broader analysis of a wide range of expressions and other linguistic devices which are also available for the expression of modality in English. The fact that the modals are syntactically distinct from other modal expressions clearly suggests that they may well be semantically distinct in some way as well, although one cannot, of course, merely assume this. It will thus be necessary to establish a framework which will enable us to assess such differences, and this will be one of the principal aims of this chapter. There are besides, however, two further aims to be achieved. Firstly, I shall try to demonstrate that it is not only feasible, but also desirable for a comparative study such as this, to isolate a core meaning for each modal. Secondly, I shall propose an analysis of the core meanings of the modals which differs in a number of ways from previous analyses.

In the account which follows, syntax will not have a central role, and this needs some initial justification. It is the traditional centrality of syntax in linguistics that has led to the modals having been singled out by linguists as the pre-eminent vehicles for the expression of modality in English, since the modals are the only modal expressions which constitute a reasonably well-defined class.[2] This has meant that the onus for establishing modal distinctions in English has had to be shouldered almost entirely by the modals, which has posed a number of problems, since all of the modals are clearly ambiguous, and this makes it at least plausible that a non-syntactic account of modality be sought. None the less, the semantic difficulties have not deterred many linguists from attempting to characterize the different uses of the modals in syntactic terms. There can be few objections to proceeding in this way if one's theoretical claims are modest and if the syntactic account is supplemented by a notional semantic analysis, as is the case with the more atheoretical treatments of the modals such as those of Ehrman (1966), Jespersen (1931), Leech (1971), Quirk *et al.* (1972), Zandvoort (1975), Palmer (1974, 1979a), and others, who are content to provide a syntactic characterization of the modals together with their various meanings in different environments. However, some of the more theoretically oriented syntactic treatments are often at pains to account for the ambiguity of the modals independently of any semantic or functional considerations, which can sometimes lead to apparent anomaly. Newmeyer (1975), for example, argues on syntactic grounds that the modals are derived from underlying intransitive structures, whereas it seems clear that, semantically at least, the modals express an inherently transitive relationship (cf. Lyons, 1977: 842, and Pullum and Wilson, 1977: 784 f.). Much of the specifically syntactic discussion of the modals in recent years has centred round issues such as whether the modals are to be regarded as main verbs (e.g. Huddleston, 1978) or as auxiliaries (e.g. Palmer, 1979b), but such discussion seems to have little direct relevance to the semantics of the modals. In view of the limitations of such syntactic accounts of modal expressions (which I have discussed at greater length elsewhere—i.e. Perkins (1980: 38 ff.)) I have found it preferable to restrict my coverage of syntax to aspects which have an obvious semantic motivation.

3.2 Core-meaning approaches to the modals

Analyses of word-meaning can usually be divided into those which assign a meaning to a word *in isolation from* a specific context of use, and those which regard the meaning of a word as being largely, if not entirely, *dependent upon* a specific context of use. The ultimate expression of the latter 'polysemantic' approach is probably that of the later Wittgenstein, who argued that 'every difference in a word's use is a consequence of and evidence for a difference in its meaning' (Wertheimer, 1972: 49). One recent example of the former 'monosemantic' approach is that of Bolinger (1977), whose stated purpose is to 'reaffirm the old principle that the natural condition of a language is to preserve one form for one meaning, and one meaning for one form' (p. x). Both these approaches have their advocates, and it should be stated at the outset that neither is necessarily right or wrong; each can be judged only according to whether the phenomena it is used to interpret are thereby illuminated.

The strategy I propose to adopt here is essentially monosemantic, in that I will try to isolate a single core meaning for each of the English modals which is independent of its context[3] of use. In choosing such a strategy, however, I accept that it cannot tell the whole story, although I *do* believe that in the case of the modals it can be particularly illuminating. Of course, such an approach is not appropriate for all linguistic expressions. It would be difficult to isolate a core meaning for the particle OF, for example, apart from saying, perhaps, that it expressed a relation of 'pertinence', but to say this does not get us very far. On the other hand, in the case of prepositions like TO, FROM, AT, etc., I think it does afford a sense of explanation to realize that the individual meaning of each preposition is essentially the same whether it is used to express a temporal or a spatial relationship. In the case of the modals in particular, there is even more to be gained by isolating a core meaning, as I will try to show.

Not just any core-meaning approach will do, however. In his recent study of modality and the English modals, Palmer (1979a: 10 ff.) gives short shrift to a number of previous 'basic meaning' approaches to the modals. Although he does not deny that we can look for a 'fairly general common meaning or a set of closely related meanings for each modal', he does suggest that 'when precision is demanded or invariance postulated . . . the notion of a basic meaning becomes unrealistic'. One can understand some of Palmer's scepticism when one considers the shortcomings of the various studies he criticizes. These range from that of Joos (1964), who attempted to represent the meanings of the modals in terms of an elegant three-dimensional matrix, to that of Bouma (1975), who defined the meanings of the modals in terms of features such as 'imminent', 'biased', and 'precarious'. Unfortunately, the elegance of Joos's account is marred by the fact that it does not accord with the intuitions of many native speakers—and this has, in fact, been experimentally verified by Emmerich (1969). The semantic primes of Bouma, on the other hand, achieve plausibility at the expense of their vagueness, which is such that 'any variations can be explained away' (Palmer, 1979a: 13).

However, there can be no *a priori* objections to core-meaning approaches to the semantics of the modals, and if the attendant dangers are kept in mind, they can be used with considerable explanatory power. But if such an approach is going to work in the case of the modals, it will clearly be necessary to ensure that the core meanings which are isolated are, on the one hand, not counter-intuitive, and on the other, are not so vague as to deny any sense of explanation.

There are, in fact, certain considerations which suggest that some kind of core-meaning approach is at least worth attempting. To propose, for example, as Huddleston (1971: 297 ff.) has done, that there are six distinct meanings of MAY, or to offer, as Kenny (1975: 131) has done, a list of 'ten distinguishable "can's" ', is to suggest that the English modal system tends more to semantic anarchy than virtually any other area of the English language. It is, furthermore, surely no mere coincidence that there are single linguistic forms which are similarly modally polysemous not only in English, but also in Amoy, Basque, Classical Aztec, French, German, Italian, Kapampangan, Korean, Luiseño, Polish, Taiwanese, Tamil, Thai, Tzeltal, Welsh, and many ancient Indo-European languages.[4] There is in addition recent psycholinguistic evidence to suggest that children between the ages of 3; 0 (i.e., 3 years and 0 months) and 6; 6 have a single lexical representation for both epistemic and deontic uses of MUST, MAY, and SHOULD (Hirst and Weil, 1982). When faced with such facts it can surely not be perverse to try and identify and account for the properties that different uses of modal expressions obviously share.

To my mind, the most promising type of core-meaning approach to the modals proposed so far is that adopted by Wertheimer in his analysis of OUGHT (Wertheimer, 1972). Wertheimer, who is interested in the philosophical implications of the modals, and of OUGHT in particular, takes the modals to be 'univocal' and describes their anomalous behaviour 'in terms, not of different senses, but of their employment in connection with various more or less independent systems of laws' (Wertheimer, 1972: 49).[5] The systems of laws which Wertheimer proposes and the various phenomena with which they interact are taken up and summarized in Miller (1978: 109) as '(a) a system K of organized belief, (b) a set of circumstances C under which the system is relevant, and (c) the consequence y that the system specifies under those circumstances'. Miller goes on to state that if the subcategorization of OUGHT is something like [NP—to VP], and 'if x is a pointer to the nominal concept expressed by NP, and y to the predicate concept expressed by VP', a lexical entry for OUGHT will contain the following semantic definition: 'OUGHT(x, y): x "ought to" y, relative to a set of circumstances C, if there is a system K such that, if C obtains, then $K \Vdash y$ [i.e. K entails y].' Note that this definition is the same whether OUGHT is used in a moral (deontic) sense or a nonmoral or inferential (epistemic) sense. The examples which Miller gives are:

21 The bell ought to ring when you close the circuit.
  i.e.:   K = the laws of electricity
       C = the fact that the bell is connected to a source of power
       y = the ringing of the bell

22 You ought to be considerate of others.
    i.e.:   K = the principles of morality
           C = personal interactions
           y = being considerate

A major advantage of such a characterization of the meaning of OUGHT is that it is not viciously circular—i.e. it is not merely a paraphrase in the sense that OUGHT = 'morally obligatory that'/ 'inferrable that' is merely a paraphrase. It makes clear that the meaning of OUGHT cannot be adequately stated without reference to variables such as K, C, y, and x. One does not have to specify the values of such variables for a particular context in order to define the core meaning of OUGHT—one simply has to specify the relationship which exists between them.

Miller's discussion of Wertheimer's treatment of OUGHT is offered simply as an illustration of a 'general strategy' one might follow in carrying out a semantic analysis of the modals, and he gives few details of how such a programme might be carried out. In 3.3 I shall develop such a strategy along my own lines in order to establish a framework which can be used for the comparative analysis of the meanings not only of the modals but of a wide range of other modal expressions as well.

3.3 The primary modals

I shall refer to CAN, MAY, MUST, WILL, and SHALL as the 'primary' modals, and to COULD, MIGHT, OUGHT TO, WOULD, and SHOULD as the 'secondary' modals. I shall not discuss DARE, which is the semantic black sheep of the modal family, and will refer to NEED only in its capacity as a suppletive form of MUST.

3.3.1 CAN

Firstly, I will point out a number of inconsistencies in several recent treatments of CAN and then suggest a way in which they may be circumvented.

In the various accounts of CAN in the linguistics literature a certain degree of confusion appears to have been generated by the fact that the same terms are sometimes used by different linguists to mean different things. The distinction between 'root' and 'epistemic' modals originally noted by Hofmann (1966) has been generally adopted in transformational treatments, but although this distinction was originally proposed as a syntactic one, there are frequent references to root and epistemic 'meanings' or 'senses' as in Collins

(1974: 154): 'In their epistemic meanings the modals express the speaker's state of knowledge or belief or opinion about the proposition. In their root senses the modals modify the surface structure subject of the sentence, indicating his volition, obligation, ability, etc.' For Collins, then, CAN would be regarded as a root modal when used in utterances expressing either permission or ability.

Pullum and Wilson (1977: 784) regard CAN as sometimes being ambiguous between a root and an epistemic interpretation and state that:

23   Elephants can kill crocodiles.

can be interpreted as either of:

23a Elephants have the ability to kill crocodiles. (Root)
23b It can happen that an elephant kills a crocodile. (Epistemic)

This is by no means a unanimously held view, however. Steele (1975: 38), for example, analyses CAN quite differently. She says that in:

24   She can swim a mile in two minutes.

the meaning of CAN (presumably, 'ability') cannot even be considered as expressing modality since it does not 'indicate the possibility of the situation which the sentence describes, but rather the potential . . . of the subject of the sentence'. For Steele, then, CAN is a root modal only when it conveys permission.

Boyd and Thorne (1969: 71 f.) hold a view similar to that of Steele in that they regard CAN as modal 'only when it is an alternative form for *may*' in its 'permission' sense. They state that there are 'at least three non-modal *cans*'—namely the CAN of ability as in:

25   He can swim over a mile.

CAN as a marker of 'progressive aspect', as in:

26   I can hear music.

and CAN as a marker of 'sporadic aspect', as in:

27   Cocktail parties can be boring.

Against this, however, Antinucci and Parisi (1971: 38) argue that such 'non-modal' uses of CAN are in fact special instances of epistemic modality in which the speaker expresses a deduction based on properties internal to the subject of the sentence.

This brief survey reveals a rather puzzling situation: CAN in its 'ability' sense has been regarded by various linguists within the space of a few years exclusively as a root modal, exclusively as an epistemic modal, and as not a modal at all!

There are a number of reasons for this apparent confusion. Firstly, few linguists have an adequate working definition of modality, and the term 'modal' is used sometimes to refer to a syntactic category and at others to a semantic category. The same is true of labels such as 'root' and 'epistemic', despite the fact that there is no straight-forward isomorphic relationship between the semantic notions and their syntactic realizations, as pointed out in 3.1. Furthermore, there has been a proliferation of terminology in the description of the modals (cf., for example, Anderson's (1971) 'non-complex vs. complex' modality, Halliday's (1970a) 'modality vs. modulation', Leech's (1971) 'factual vs. theoretical' modality and Young's (1980) 'knowledge vs. influence' modality) and this seems to be symptomatic of the difficulty linguists experience in discussing the meanings of the modals; and, as we have seen, those terms which *are* commonly used are often given different nuances by different linguists.

My aim here will be to avoid the loose and often inconsistent types of labelling system noted above by basing my description of modal expressions on the definition of modality proposed in 2.1. As my first step, in the remainder of this subsection I shall argue that the polysemy of CAN is a function of the contexts in which it occurs, and that the disagreement apparent in the treatments referred to above may be resolved by postulating a core meaning for CAN which may be represented as a relationship between three variables whose values (which are specified contextually) on any given occasion determine the way in which CAN will be interpreted.

Palmer, in *The English Verb* (Palmer, 1974: 115 ff.), describes the use of CAN in:

28 He can lift a hundredweight.
29 I can see the moon.
30 He can tell awful lies.

as follows: in (28) it is the 'CAN of ability', in (29) the 'CAN of sensation', and in (30) 'characteristic CAN'. In other words, CAN is to be regarded as having three different meanings or uses. It is significant, however, that if we add AT TIMES to (28) and (29), they too can support a 'characteristic' interpretation, and it would appear, therefore, that in such cases the 'characteristicness' is due, if not to the expression AT TIMES itself, then at most to the co-occurrence of CAN and AT TIMES.[6] Thus Palmer is, in fact, describing the meaning of sentences rather than the meaning of CAN and his method of labelling is not, therefore, entirely accurate.

One might object, however, that in (30) a 'characteristic' interpretation is possible even though no such expression as AT TIMES is present. The answer to this is that in (30) the 'characteristicness' still has little to do with CAN but is due to the nature of the activity referred to—namely that of telling awful lies—which is typically seen as a recurrent phenomenon, thus:

31 He tells awful lies.

is just as 'characteristic' as (30), even though CAN is absent.

A further complication here is that in some contexts it is even possible to regard the activity of telling lies as an ability, rather than a characteristic. Consider the following, for example:

32 He'd make a good confidence trickster—he can tell awful lies with the most innocent expression.

Palmer's method of analysis would presumably lead him to interpret CAN in (32) as an instance of the 'CAN of ability', rather than of 'characteristic CAN'.

Palmer further claims that 'characteristic CAN' often has a derogatory sense, and as evidence cites:

33 She can be very catty at times.

However, the derogatoriness of (33) again has little to do with CAN, since it is also possible to say things like:

34 She can be very charming at times.

Similar observations are possible with (29): the 'sensation' interpretation is due to the presence of a verb of sensation—e.g. SEE, HEAR, SMELL, FEEL, TASTE—with which CAN co-occurs.

Clearly, what Palmer is doing is giving an account of some of the possible environments of CAN, rather than of CAN itself, but this seems to bypass the question of what CAN itself actually contributes to the meaning of a sentence. To get some idea of what its contribution might be, consider the difference between:

35 Joan can hear voices telling her to save France.
36 Joan hears voices telling her to save France.

which are cited by Lakoff (1972a). Lakoff states that in (35) 'it is assumed that the speaker agrees with Joan that the voices are real'. In (36), on the other hand, she says 'they may be hallucinations'. Now although I would not entirely agree with this comment, I think one could certainly say that there is more apparent speaker involvement in (35) than in (36). In (36) the speaker is simply asserting the proposition 'Joan hears voices telling her to save France'. This is the type of assertion frequently used in commentaries where the commentator does not want to intrude his or her own viewpoint. In (35), on the other hand, the speaker seems 'to be implying that circumstances exist which make it possible for Joan to hear voices telling her to save France, and such circumstances may well include the voices themselves.

As a further illustration of this, consider:

37   Footballers can be sex maniacs.

which is also quoted by Lakoff (1972a: 230) and which she says she would utter only 'in case [she] knew positively of at least one instance in which at least one football player had acted like a sex maniac'. Such an instance counts as part of a set of circumstances which are seen as relevant to the occurrence of the event referred to in the propositional content of the utterance, and some such circumstance must clearly be recoverable if CAN is to be used felicitously.

The contribution of CAN to the meaning of a sentence seems to be, therefore, roughly, to relate the event referred to in the propositional content to some external circumstance which is not explicitly identified but whose existence is presupposed, and the precise relationship between the circumstance and the event appears to be that the nature of the circumstance is not such as to preclude the event occurring. (Such a meaning is clearly related to the notion of possibility, but it is important to note that possibility is being represented here as a transitive relationship between circumstances and an event (cf. Lyons, 1977: 843 f.), rather than as an intransitive concept, as is more frequently the case.) To show this a little more clearly we can compare the following categorical assertion:

38   John swims.

with a modalized version:

39   John can swim.

In (38) the speaker categorically asserts that John swims. This might be represented as:

38a   Speaker⟶Assert⟶John swim

In (39), however, it is not actually asserted that John swims, but merely that there are circumstances which are not such as to preclude such an eventuality. This might be represented as:

Circumstances exist which do not preclude

39a   Speaker ⟶ Assert   ↘John swim

Note that in (39a) the speaker's assertory commitment is diverted away from the event itself and towards some circumstance to which the event is merely made relative. CAN—and, as we shall see later, all modal expressions—could thus in a sense be regarded as a realization of a semantic system which intervenes between the speaker and some aspect of the objective world.

This information, however, is still insufficient to enable CAN to be used effectively or to be properly understood. In addition, the use of CAN involves a set of laws or principles according to which the relationship between circumstance and event can be interpreted. In examples (28) to (39), the relevant set of principles seems to be akin to the laws of nature, or natural laws, which were discussed in 2.1 (cf. also Harre, 1959: 49). For example, if we utter (39), we may have in mind some set of circumstances which includes, say, a previous occasion on which John demonstrated his ability to swim, and which is certainly not such as to preclude a similar occurrence happening again, should an appropriate occasion arise. We may thus represent the meaning of CAN in such cases by means of the following formula:

40   K (C does not preclude that e occur)
      where: i.   K = natural laws
              ii. C = an empirical circumstance
              iii. e = an event
              iv. K(x) = x is the case relative to K

When used in this sense, CAN expresses dynamic modality—i.e. it is concerned with the disposition of certain empirical circumstances with regard to the occurrence of some event (cf. the discussion of dynamic modality in 2.1).

In addition to its dynamic possibility sense, since about the eighteenth century it has also been possible to use CAN in the sense of deontic possibility—i.e. permission (cf. Traugott, 1972: 198)—as in:

41   You can go now.
42   Can I borrow this pen, please?
43   If you don't eat your meat, you can't have any pudding.

In this case, K would represent the laws of society, or social laws (cf. 2.1) and C would involve what Lyons (1977: 843) has called a 'deontic source'—i.e. a person or institution which creates a permission or obligation.

There are also cases where CAN might be regarded as having an epistemic sense, as in:

44 There can only be one outcome of nuclear war.
45 Cigarettes can seriously damage your health.

—that is, K will represent rational laws (e.g. inference, deduction) (cf. 2.1) and C will represent evidence which is not such as to preclude the truth of a proposition p. At the same time, however, it is also possible to regard such examples as expressing dynamic modality (i.e. K = natural laws, C = an event) and thus the decision is not clear-cut. The indeterminacy of such cases depends on what set of laws is thought to be most appropriate and whether one feels one is dealing with empirical circumstances as empirical circumstances, or else as evidence from which the truth status of a proposition may be inferred, and it is just possible that the speakers of (44) and (45) could intend both at the same time. At any rate, no matter what the values of K and C might be in a particular context, it is still possible to represent the core meaning of CAN as:

46 K (C does not preclude X)

where X is a variable which may represent the occurrence of an event under a dynamic or deontic interpretation and the truth of a proposition under an epistemic interpretation. The semantic parallel which exists between dynamic, deontic, and epistemic uses of CAN, as captured by (46), helps to explain why a single form is used in the service of different meanings, and the semantic structure of CAN as shown here may thus be regarded as the meaning which is common to CAN in all its uses. By postulating such an invariant core meaning for CAN which can interact with one or more of three different systems of laws according to its context of use, it is possible to show that many of the problems connected with giving an adequate semantic definition of CAN (such as its alleged polysemy and semantic indeterminacy) may be plausibly regarded as contextual, and that questions about whether particular instances of CAN should be interpreted as dynamic, deontic, or epistemic need not be resolved by postulating a set of three distinct lexical items which happen to share the same formal realization.

There is still a good deal more to be said about CAN—in particular we need to consider whether there are any constraints upon the possible values of its semantic variables—but this can best be

shown by contrasting the meaning of CAN with those of the other
primary modals which are discussed in 3.3.2 and 3.3.3.

3.3.2 MAY and MUST[7]

It is widely recognized that MAY and MUST can be used in either
a deontic or an epistemic sense, as can be seen in the suggested
readings of the following examples:

A. *Deontic*:
47 You must never breath a word of this.
48 You must call in and see us some time.
49 You may leave the table when everyone has finished.
50 May I have a quick word with you?
B. *Epistemic*:
51 Why, you must be Dr. Livingstone!
52 They must have used their pass keys to get in.
53 This may be the last cigarette I smoke.
54 I may have left it in the car.

As in the case with CAN, however, MAY and MUST are often
regarded as being highly polysemous. Huddleston (1971: 297 ff.),
for example, who suggests a number of different meanings for each
of the modals, distinguishes six different uses of MAY, which I
reproduce here with an example of each:

a. *Qualified generalization*: 'The reproductive cells *may* encyst
    themselves and it has been suggested on this evidence . . . '
b. *Exhaustive disjunction*: 'These anemones *may* be blue or dull
    green . . . '
c. *Uncertainty*: 'The study of luminescence . . . *may* provide a
    valuable test for long-distance geological prospecting . . . '
d. *Concession*: 'Whatever the relations *may* be, . . . '
e. *Legitimacy*: 'This lacuna in our knowledge of the sea *may*
    be attributed in a large part to . . . '
f. *Ability*: 'It *may* be shown that . . . '

   What Huddleston has done here is to find a paraphrase for MAY
in each environment and to turn it into a label for a category of
use. His six subcategories of uses of MAY are based on pragmatic
inferences from the context of use and semantic clues present in
the rest of the sentence, but all of these different uses can be
accounted for in a less *ad hoc* manner by relating a core meaning
to a limited set of laws. As is the case with CAN, the core meanings
of MAY and MUST can both be represented as a relationship between
the variables K, C, and X as follows:

55 MUST: K(C entails X)[8]
56 MAY: K(C does not preclude X)[9]
   where: i. K = social laws/rational laws (typically)
          ii. C = deontic source/evidence (typically)
          iii. X = the occurrence of e/the truth of p

It is typically the case that an utterance containing a deontic use of MAY (and also CAN for that matter) will be used to express permission, although there are apparent exceptions. For example:

57 You may go.

uttered by someone in a position of authority to someone of much lower authority would probably be understood as a command. This, however, is entirely due to the circumstances peculiar to such a situation. If the same person had said:

58 You may smoke.

for example, it would probably be understood not as a command but as a giving of permission. Such pragmatic factors may override, but are nevertheless quite separate from, the core meaning of MAY.

The fact that MAY has been represented as having the same core meaning as CAN obviously needs some explanation. Although the core meanings of CAN and MAY can both be characterized in the same way, the two expressions differ in that each has a different set of constraints on the possible values of K, C, and X.[10] Whereas CAN most typically relates to natural or social laws (i.e. dynamic and deontic modality), MAY most typically relates to rational or social laws (i.e. epistemic and deontic modality), although, as we have seen, CAN may sometimes appear to relate to rational laws and MAY, as we shall see, sometimes appears to relate to natural laws. In cases where it is possible to interpret MAY in a dynamic sense, such as:

59 We may now move on to the next question.

or in the following two attested examples quoted by Palmer:

60 Cader Idris, however, may be climbed from other points on this tour.
61 Where, in a secluded valley in the west, you may find the neat little Norman church of Pennant Melangell.

CAN might easily be substituted for MAY, although the effect of this would be to render the examples slightly less formal. When MAY, as it were impinges on CAN's dynamic territory in this way, either the hypotheticality of its epistemic use or the permission sense of its deontic use never appears to be far away, and this has the effect of differentiating the examples with MAY from the more purely dynamic versions with CAN in such a way that MAY in such contexts has come to be conventionally regarded as more polite or formal than CAN.

A similar distinction is apparent when CAN encroaches upon MAY's deontic territory—an encroachment which, as was noted in 3.3.1, dates only from the eighteenth century.[11] The comparatively recent development of the deontic use of CAN has meant that until quite recently it has been fashionable for popular grammar books to state that it is incorrect to use CAN to express permission,[12] and this view is still widely held, though not entirely consistently, as can be seen in this example cited by Marino (1973: 320):

62 Johnny: 'Can I go out?'
   Mother: 'Not *can, may*.'
   Johnny: 'O.K., may I go out?'
   Mother: 'Sure you can.'

However, the deontic use of CAN is now well established and prejudices seem to have weakened to the point where CAN is no longer regarded as incorrect, but merely as a less polite version of MAY. Thus MAY would typically be regarded as more polite than CAN in examples like:

63 May I speak to the manager, please?
64 Can I speak to the manager, please?[13]

The inroads made by CAN into MAY's epistemic territory, on the other hand, are far less substantial and some (e.g. Palmer, 1979a: 157) would dispute whether any inroads had been made at all. The reasons for this appear to be as follows. Firstly, the epistemic use of MAY indicates that evidence available to the speaker is such that the proposition expressed by the sentence cannot currently be inferred to be true, but nor can it currently be inferred to be false. CAN, on the other hand, in its central dynamic sense is not directly concerned with the truth of propositions but rather with the disposition of circumstances *vis-à-vis* the occurrence of some event. CAN focuses primarily on the current state of circumstances, whereas epistemic MAY focuses primarily on the current verifiability of the truth of a proposition. Hence one can say:

65 John can run a four-minute mile, but he never will because he's too lazy.

but not:

66 *John may run a four-minute mile, but he never will because he's too lazy.

(66) is unacceptable because it cites evidence that the proposition 'John run a four-minute mile' is currently falsifiable, whereas MAY indicates that it is neither currently verifiable or falsifiable. In (65), on the other hand, it is irrelevant whether John actually will run a four-minute mile or not, as long as circumstances are currently not such as to preclude it.

However, there are contexts in which the use of CAN does make it possible to make claims about the current verifiability of the expressed proposition. In:

67 I can hear music.

(i.e. an example of what Boyd and Thorne (1969: 72) regard as the 'progressive aspectual' use of CAN), for example, the circumstance which does not preclude the occurrence of my hearing music is presumably the fact of my actually hearing music, which means, therefore, that one can infer that the proposition 'I hear music' is currently true. It follows more generally that on any occasion when CAN is used dynamically and the relevant circumstance is currently recoverable from the context of utterance, then the (set of) proposition(s) referring to that circumstance will be currently true. For example, if I know that John thinks Mary is a rather plain-looking girl and yet on a particular occasion when Mary turns up at a party looking atypically stunning I hear John say:

68 My! Mary can be attractive, can't she!

I may reasonably infer that John currently believes the proposition 'Mary is attractive' to be true.

Now such a feature is clearly not attributable to the core meaning of CAN, but is entirely due to a particular context of use; but it does mean that in certain cases a dynamic use of CAN may also permit an epistemic interpretation, and in the case of the use of CAN with verbs of sensation, it is the epistemic interpretation which has come, apparently by convention, to predominate. As Palmer (1974: 117) has noted in comparing:

69 I see the moon.
70 I can see the moon.

'the modal seems . . . to add nothing that is not indicated by the non-modal form' and he suggests in a later work (Palmer, 1979a: 74 f.) that the use of CAN with verbs of sensation 'is an idiomatic use, one that has no further explanation'. However, the above account does appear to offer a plausible explanation of this particular use of CAN which relates it to its use in less idiomatic contexts.

One significant consequence of the indirect epistemic reading of CAN in (70) is that instead of expressing a relationship of 'non-preclusion' between C (evidence) and X (the truth of p), it expresses a relationship of entailment—i.e. under an indirect epistemic reading CAN appears to mean 'relative to K (rational laws) C (evidence) entails X (the truth of p)', although it must be stressed that with the possible exception of its use with verbs of sensation, such a reading is only an indirect consequence of a dynamic reading under exceptional circumstances. The reading of CAN in this indirect epistemic sense is, of course, the same as that of MUST in its direct epistemic sense, and it is interesting that the very circumstances which enable an epistemic reading of (70) make an epistemic reading of:

71 I must see the moon. (?)

decidedly odd.

It is relevant in this context to recall the frequently recorded fact that for many speakers CAN'T is a much more natural expression than epistemic MUSTN'T,[14] which Lyons (1977: 802) takes as evidence for the view that 'in English at least, possibility, rather than necessity, should be taken as primitive in the analysis of epistemic modality'.

A further difference between dynamic/deontic CAN and deontic/dynamic MAY is that the former may be what Palmer (1974: 100) calls 'subject-oriented'—i.e. it may 'relate semantically to some kind of activity, quality, status, etc. of the subject of the sentence', whereas MAY is never subject-oriented. (Cf. also Anderson's (1971: 89 ff.) distinction between 'internal' and 'external' modals and Halliday's (1970a: 339) distinction between 'active modulation' and 'passive modulation'.) In the present account, this phenomenon may be represented as a constraint on the possible values of the C variable such that in the case of CAN, C may represent either some circumstance which originates within, but need not be under the conscious control of, the referent of the subject of the sentence, as in:

72 He can speak fourteen languages.
73 What can you contribute to the discussion?

or else some circumstance which originates outside the referent of the subject, as in:

74 You can go now, thank you.
75 She can be the bus driver and I can be the ambulance driver.

With MAY, on the other hand, the state of affairs represented by C is always external to the referent of the subject—cf.:

76 He may speak fourteen languages.
77 What may you contribute to the discussion? (?)

It appears from the above discussion that CAN and MAY may plausibly be regarded as contextually determined formal variants which realize the same core meaning—namely, K(C does not preclude X). The major realizational constraints on K(C does not preclude X) are that it will typically be realized as CAN if one or more of the following hold:

a. K = natural laws/C = empirical circumstances
b. K = social laws/C = a deontic source (informal context)
c. C is subject-oriented
d. X denotes a characteristic

and as MAY if one or more of the following hold:

e. K = rational laws/C = evidence
f. K = social laws/C = a deontic source (formal context)
g. K = natural laws/C = empirical circumstances (formal context)

There are, in addition, a number of syntactic constraints (some of which will be discussed in 3.3.4), which, although often inadequate in isolation to ensure that one or the other form is realized, will often tip the balance either way in conjunction with one or more of (a) to (g). It is not my aim, however, to provide an exhaustive account of all pragmatic, semantic, and syntactic constraints relating to CAN and MAY or any of the other modals,[15] but merely to demonstrate how such constraints may be accounted for in terms of a set of variables with a limited range of values, which also, incidentally, provide a framework for describing the diachronic instability of the modals.

The constraints on MUST as a realization of the core meaning K(C entails X) are similar to those proposed for MAY, although with MUST there are no formality contrasts with other members of the modal auxiliary system. It should be noted, however, that K(C entails X) is realized as NEED in interrogative environments and where X is negated (cf. 3.3.4). One further point is that it is commonly believed that MUST is subject-oriented. There are, however, occasional exceptions, such as:

78 You must go poking your nose into everything!

where MUST means something like 'insist' and the deontic source is
clearly intrinsic to the referent of the subject.

3.3.3 WILL and SHALL

A vast amount has been written about WILL and SHALL, and yet
there are a number of conflicting views which are still sometimes
hotly disputed (cf., for example, Palmer (1978) vs. Huddleston
(1979)). In this section I will suggest a basis for resolving some of
these disputes.

One long-standing debate is about whether WILL and SHALL
should be regarded primarily as future-tense morphemes (as argued
by Scheurweghs (1959: 333), Sweet (1898: 97), Wekker (1976),
Zandvoort (1975: 76), and many others) or as modal auxiliary verbs
(as argued, for example, by Fries (1927: 94), Jespersen (1924:
260), Joos (1964: 120), Lyons (1968: 306), McIntosh (1966: 304),
Palmer (1974: 36 f.), Quirk *et al.* (1972: 87), and Rudin (1977:
14 ff.)). There now appears, however, to be sufficient evidence, both
diachronic (cf. Lyons, 1977: 816 ff.) and based on a wide variety of
other languages (cf. Ultan, 1972), to give strong support to the view
that the use of WILL and SHALL to refer to future time is secondary
to a more modal function. The view that will be proposed here is
that WILL and SHALL are both realizations of the same core meaning—namely:

79 K(C is disposed towards X)

which may be used in epistemic, deontic, and dynamic contexts.[16]
The precise meaning of 'C is disposed towards X' in (79) may be
better understood by comparing it with that of 'C does not preclude
X'. In the latter case, neither X nor not-X is a logical consequence of
C—i.e. C has neither a positive nor a negative bias towards X. In 'C
is disposed towards X', on the other hand, although it is likewise the
case that neither X nor its negation is entailed by C, there is a definite
bias towards X as opposed to not-X, and 'disposed' in (79) should be
understood in the sense of 'positively disposed'. 'C is disposed
towards X', therefore, lies somewhere between 'C does not preclude
X' and 'C entails X'.[17]

The more typical view of WILL and SHALL is that they have a
wide range of meanings with no common basis. Palmer (1979a),
for example, deals with WILL under the separate headings of 'volition', 'power', 'habit', 'futurity', 'conditionality', and 'epistemic'.
One attempt to isolate a core meaning for WILL is that of Boyd and

Thorne (1969) who state (pp. 63 f.): 'the only function of the modal verb *will* is to indicate that the illocutionary potential of the sentence in which it occurs is that of being a prediction'. However, although this is plausible for many uses of WILL, it does not easily (if at all) account for the use of WILL in 'volitional' contexts such as:

80 Will you lend me your car, please?
81 Jim won't let anyone near him.

It is absurd to suggest that the speaker of (80) is asking his addressee to make a prediction regarding his future behaviour, or that (81) is simply a prediction about Jim's future behaviour. Apparently to get round objections such as this, Boyd and Thorne state in a footnote (p. 64) that WILL in examples like (80) and (81) is not a modal verb at all, but merely a homonym of modal WILL; but this would appear to be a rather arbitrary ruling.

It is also suggested by Boyd and Thorne (1969: 65) that 'the illocutionary force of utterances with SHALL is that of being a demand that the speaker makes of himself', but this is certainly not true in cases like:

82 If the train is late, I shall miss my connection.

where the speaker could hardly be said to be demanding of himself that he miss his connection.

Antinucci and Parisi (1971) propose an analysis of WILL that likens it to MUST, and as a means of distinguishing between the two state (p. 38) that: 'it seems to us that the difference between the [epistemic] use of *must* and the [epistemic] use of *will* . . . lies precisely in that sentences with *must* always imply reference to a causing event, while this is not true of simple sentences containing epistemic *will*'.[18] However, this does not tie in very well with their analysis of 'root' WILL, as in:

83 You must do as you're told.
84 You will do as you're told.

The use of WILL in commands like (84) is almost certainly a conventional implication from its dynamic use (or more specifically its boulomaic use—i.e. where the circumstance referred to by C is a property of human consciousness (cf. 2.1)).[19] Traugott (1972: 199) suggests that the nearest WILL has ever come to the expression of obligation is where it is used to express 'resolve'. According to the results of an experiment conducted by Mohan (1974) to assess attitudes to the relative politeness of different linguistic forms, the utterance of:

85 You will open the door.

was regarded as less polite than:

86 You must open the door.

in a situation where the addressee is an acquaintance (not a close friend) of the same age and sex as the speaker, and is sitting on the opposite side of the room. A possible reason for this is that (85) is regarded as being nearer to a direct assertion than (86) which, according to Mohan, would correspond to a proportional difference in politeness.

The view being proposed here, then, is that although (84) and (85) could certainly be interpreted as expressing deontic modality, this appears to be secondary to a more central use of WILL to express boulomaic modality.

There is also further evidence that MUST as used in (83) differs considerably from WILL as used in (84) and from SHALL as used in:

87 You shall do as you're told.

If I SAY SO is tagged on to any of these three sentences, they are all still acceptable. If HE SAYS SO is tagged on, however, (84) and (87) appear odd unless they are taken to be a direct quotation of the actual words spoken. WILL and SHALL cannot, in fact, be used to report another person's directive. If someone utters (84) or (87) as a directive, this will normally be reported by one of:

88 X says you must do as you're told.
89 X says you've got to do as you're told.
90 X says you're to do as you're told.

MUST (and also MAY and CAN for that matter), on the other hand, *can* be used to report another person's directive. It is not immediately clear, in fact, whether (83) is to be regarded as a direct or an indirect directive: it is compatible with either interpretation, and only the context of utterance will enable a decision to be made one way or the other. Thus MUST can express deontic modality whether the utterance which incorporates it is a statement or a command. WILL and SHALL, on the other hand, can be interpreted deontically only if the utterance which incorporates them can itself be construed as a deontic source, and the social laws invoked will always be concerned with differences in role or status between the speaker and addressee, as opposed to formal institutional laws. The fact that the deontic source exists by virtue of the personal authority of the speaker accounts for the sense of 'speaker's guarantee' noted by

Boyd and Thorne (1969: 95), Palmer (1979a: 62), Haegeman (1981), and others.

In the case of Boyd and Thorne's thesis that WILL = 'prediction' —i.e. that WILL expresses epistemic modality—it can also be argued that WILL primarily expresses dynamic (but in this case non-boulomaic) modality but may also have an epistemic sense under certain circumstances. If we compare:

91 You must be John's daughter.
92 You will be John's daughter.

the speaker of (91) clearly seems to be aware of evidence which, for him and according to rational laws, entails the truth of the proposition 'Addressee be John's daughter'. With (92), on the other hand, there need not be any such conclusive evidence: circumstances are merely disposed towards the addressee's being John's daughter. However, if such a disposition is taken to be *evidence* which has some bearing on the truth of the expressed proposition, then an epistemic interpretation is possible. According to this analysis, there can be no set of foolproof objective rules for determining whether a given use of WILL is necessarily dynamic or epistemic (although certainly one or the other interpretation might appear more plausible in specific contexts), for it is quite possible to regard a case like (92) as epistemic and dynamic at the same time, depending on the perspective one feels inclined to take.

To show how the analysis of the core meaning of WILL (SHALL will be dealt with in more detail nearer the end of this section) as K(C is disposed towards X) appears to underlie all its uses, I will now briefly examine how it relates to the various different headings used by Palmer which were mentioned above, and I will also borrow some of his attested examples.

When WILL is used to express 'volition', as in:

93 I said 'Why don't you go and see if Martin will let you stay?'

or 'power' as in:

94 You know that certain drugs will improve the condition.

it is always subject-oriented. In other words, the circumstance referred to by C is seen as being intrinsic to the referent of the subject of WILL. Both are examples of dynamic modality, although the 'volitional' use, unlike the 'power' use, specifically expresses boulomaic modality.

In 'habit' uses of WILL, such as:

95 So one kid will say to another, one kid will make a suggestion to
    another, he'll say the moon's further away from the earth than
    the sun.

and in 'futurity' uses, such as:

96 They'll be company for you, and whereas other old women
    might be terribly lonely, you will never be lonely.

C refers simply to unspecified empirical circumstances.
    In conditional sentences, such as:

97 If he feels like doing it, that'll save me the trouble.

the identity of C is specified in the IF-clause.
    Palmer's final heading, 'epistemic', has already been dealt with
above.
    In every case, the identification of the referent of C—i.e. the
source of the disposition—will usually be sufficient to determine
the precise way in which a given instance of WILL is to be understood.
    It is now necessary to specify the conditions under which K(C is
disposed towards X) is realized as SHALL, as opposed to WILL, but
first two preliminary points need to be made. Historically, the meanings of WILL and SHALL are quite distinct. According to Strang
(1970: 203 f.), during the period from 1370 to 1570 SHALL meant
'I must, am under obligation to' and WILL meant 'I want to, will'.
This distinction has been somewhat eroded, however, and today the
situation is quite different. For one thing, SHALL is considerably
rarer than WILL in modern English, being restricted (in informal
speech at least) largely to first person interrogatives.[20,21] Ehrman
(1966: 56) concludes from a study of a 300,000 word corpus of
contemporary written American English that 'shall is most likely to
be a stylistic device expressing the same basic meaning as that of
will but also reflecting a quantity of formal education which the
writer wants to show'.
    In modern English the status of SHALL seems to be purely that of
a suppletive form of WILL which is used either in contexts where
WILL might seem ambiguous or as a more formal variant. In first
person interrogatives, SHALL is used instead of WILL to indicate
that it is the addressee's disposition which is being referred to, as
opposed to the speaker's—cf.:

98 Will I go?
99 Shall I go?

(although this distinction is not valid in Scottish English, for example, where WILL is used in both senses (cf. Trudgill and Hannah, 1982)). In first person indicative environments, SHALL is used instead of WILL, in both volitional and non-volitional contexts, in order to convey an air of formality. Compare the following, for example:

100 I will do as I like.[22] (non-formal)
101 I shall do as I like. (formal) } volitional
102 I will be met by Mr. Dean. (non-formal)
103 I shall be met by Mr. Dean. (formal) } non-volitional

(Cf. also the frequent use of SHALL in official documents.)

In second and third person non-interrogative environments where a deontic reading is possible, SHALL may also be used to convey formality, as in:

104 You will get your own supper! (non-formal)
105 You shall get your own supper! (formal)
106 They will not set foot in this house! (non-formal)
107 They shall not set foot in this house! (formal)

In cases such as (105) and (107), SHALL might be thought to have retained part of its original meaning, in that SHALL is unambiguously deontic whereas WILL is not, although another less diachronically oriented view would be that SHALL is used in such cases as a marked version of WILL to indicate that it is the speaker's disposition which is involved, as opposed to that of the addressee, of the referent of the subject, or of objective circumstances, in situations where WILL might have been ambiguous.

It is clearly reasonable to argue, therefore, that WILL and SHALL are contextually determined formal variants which realize a common core meaning.

3.3.4 The primary modals and negation

In terms of a definition of modality such as that of Rescher (1968: 24) quoted in 2.1—namely that 'when ... a proposition is ... made subject to some further qualification of such a kind that the entire resulting complex is itself once again a proposition, then this quali-fication is said to represent a *modality* to which the original proposi-tion is subjected'—it would also be possible to regard negation as a modality. Furthermore, from a conceptualist perspective, to conceive of a state of affairs not being the case when it is the case, or to conceive of a proposition not being true when in fact it is true, is to envisage a possible world which is not cohomologous with the actual world. It is also, perhaps, worth noting that Kruisinga

(1932: 527) refers to NOT and N'T as 'adverbs of modality'. However, if negation *is* a type of modality, it is a somewhat idiosyncratic type, since rather than simply qualifying, it transforms, and to talk of the negation of a proposition in terms of the truth of the proposition being made relative to its falsity, or of the negation of an event in terms of the occurrence of the event being made relative to its non-occurrence, is somewhat odd. For the purposes of the present account, therefore, I will consider negation to be an independent semantic system which merely interacts with modality.

It is well known that modal expressions provide some of the clearest evidence for the phenomena usually referred to as 'external' and 'internal' negation.[23] The difference between the two can be seen in the semantic non-equivalence of:

108 It's not possible that pigs fly.
109 It's possible that pigs don't fly.

In (108) the modality is negated, while in (109) the proposition itself is negated. Similar distinctions are observable with the modals as well. The following:

110 Pigs can't fly.
111 Pigs may not fly.

are in some contexts equivalent to (108) and (109) respectively, and it is thus the case that negation, in conjunction with the type of modality to be expressed, is one of the factors which will determine which realization of a core meaning may be used in cases where more than one realization is available. The 'effect of negation on the modals has been extensively discussed (cf., for example, Anderson (1971: 97 ff.), Coates (1983), Greenbaum (1974), Leech (1971: 87 ff.), Palmer (1974: 131 ff., 137 ff., and 1979a)), although it is not always regarded as a contextual constraint upon a core meaning.

Within the framework proposed above, the effect of negation upon the core meanings of the primary modals may be represented as follows:

a. CAN'T/CANNOT: K(C precludes X)[24]
b. CAN NÒT: K(C does not preclude not-X)
c. MAY NOT (epistemic): ⎫
d. MAY NÒT (deontic):   ⎬ K(C does not preclude not-X)
e. MAY NOT (deontic): K(C precludes X)[24]
f. NEEDN'T/NEED NOT (deontic/epistemic): K(C does not entail X)
g. MUSTN'T/MUST NOT (deontic/epistemic: K(C entails not-X)
h. WON'T/WILL NOT: ⎫
i. SHAN'T/SHALL NOT: ⎬ K(C is disposed towards not-X

Some examples of the above are:

a(i)   That *can't* be Dr. Livingstone!
a(ii) I *cannot* abide deceit.
b(i)   If you don't feel up to it you *can* always *nòt* go.
c(i)   It may be Dr. Livingstone—but then again it *may not.*
d(i)   In view of the printing error, the exam board has agreed that you *may nòt* answer the third question.
e(i)   You *may not* start until I tell you.
f(i)   You *needn't* answer that question.
f(ii) He *needn't* be Dr. Livingstone.
g(i)   You *mustn't* reveal what I've said on any account.
g(ii) He *must not* be Dr. Livingstone after all.
h(i)   I *won't* hear a word of it.
h(ii) You *won't* have curly hair unless you eat your crusts.
i(i)   We *shan't* be late after all.
i(ii) They *shall not* pass.

There are a number of points to be made here. Firstly, when the modality is negated in K(C entails X), this is realized as NEEDN'T or NEED NOT, as opposed to MUSTN'T or MUST NOT, which is used only when the proposition/event is negated. The equivalence of K(C precludes X) and K(C entails not-X) accounts for the reason why CAN'T may be used as a suppletive of MUST in negative epistemic contexts. (b) and (d) are possible only in a context where some kind of explicit or implicit contrast with the negated-modality form is present.

The representation of (h) and (i) is not definitive. It is sometimes pointed out (e.g. by Halliday, 1970a: 332, and Palmer, 1974: 137) that it makes no difference in the case of WILL whether we regard the modality or proposition/event as being negated, but such a judgement depends on what paraphrases of WILL are used in the explanation. Both Halliday and Palmer base their decisions on the assumed equivalence of WON'T with both IT IS NOT PROBABLE THAT and IT IS PROBABLE THAT NOT, but it will be shown in 5.4 that there are important semantic differences between WILL and PROBABLE THAT. It may appear that h(i) and i(ii) could better be represented as K(C is not disposed towards X), but it should be remembered that the expression IS DISPOSED TOWARDS is also a paraphrase and that it permits transferred negation (cf. 5.4), which means that although the negative operator appears before the verb, it is still, logically, the proposition/event which is negated. Since paraphrasing is the only formal means of arriving at a decision on the matter, I will leave the question open, and the representation given for (h) and (i) should be taken as representing nothing more than my own subjective judgement.

3.4 The secondary modals

The difference which will be proposed here between the primary
modals CAN, MAY, MUST, WILL, and SHALL and the secondary
modals COULD, MIGHT, OUGHT TO, WOULD, and SHOULD is
that the latter all share a common semantic feature which is not
present, at least in the same degree, in the former. Although this
feature is semantically identical for each secondary modal, it may
have a number of different interpretations, depending on the context
of utterance in which it occurs. It may, for example, be used as an
index of hypothesis, temporal reference, formality, politeness, or
tentativeness, and often more than one of these at the same time.
It would probably be more accurate to represent such a feature as
being locatable at a point on one of the following pragmatic scales:

    non-hypothetical——————————hypothetical
           non-past——————————past
          non-formal——————————formal
          non-polite——————————polite
        non-tentative——————————tentative
        non-indirect——————————indirect

where each scale may be regarded as a different interpretative domain
for the feature in question. In some cases the meanings of the primary modals may also be interpreted in terms of certain of these
scales (e.g. 'He may be mad' is more tentative than 'He is mad'),
but whenever this is so, the secondary modals will always be to the
right of their primary counterparts (e.g. 'He might be mad' is more
tentative than 'He may be mad') and the degree of separation will
be due to the semantic feature referred to above. This feature, in
so far as it is recognized as such, has been variously described in
terms of its pragmatic correlates in particular contexts of utterance.
Jespersen (1931: 112), for example, speaks of the 'imaginative use
of tenses'; Halliday (1970a: 334) refers to modification by 'undertone
or overtone'; Palmer (1974: 127) states that the secondary modals
are used to express tentativeness. However, there appears to be a
generalization being missed here through the overemphasis of what
can be taken to be a single semantic distinction. All of the scales
given above—and the list is not necessarily exhaustive—can be sub-
sumed under the single scale:

    non-conditional——————————conditional

because all presuppose that there is a particular condition, or
conditioning environment, present in the context of utterance.[25]

Sometimes the condition will be realized formally as a conditional clause, and sometimes it will merely be left implicit in the context of utterance; but no matter what its formal status might be, such a condition must always be present in some way or another if there is a conditional feature formally explicit within the utterance.

By way of example I will first look at the way in which WOULD can be seen to be more 'conditional' than WILL. Consider the use of WOULD in:

112 I *would* read more if I had the time. (hypothetical)
113 Before the new bus service started, he *would* catch the 8 o'clock train. (past)
114 He *would* keep on all the time. (past emphatic)
115 *Would* Mr. Smith come to the information desk? (formal)
116 *Would* you pass the harissa, please? (polite)
117 *Would* you be Dr. Livingstone? (tentative)
118 He said he *would* be there. (indirect)

The terms in parentheses suggest a pragmatic reading for each sentence.

The only examples where the conditional environments are formally explicit are (112)—namely 'if I had the time'[26]—and (118) —namely 'he said'—although such environments could easily have been realized pragmatically instead. (113) incorporates what is usually called something like the 'past habitual' use of WOULD. It can be understood as an instance of disposition conditioned by a past time environment. That is, during a particular period in the past, and prior to certain specific instances of such an occurrence, circumstances were disposed to X's catching the 8 o'clock train. USED TO is often regarded as a synonym of this use of WOULD (and is sometimes even regarded as a modal auxiliary—cf. Quirk *et al.* 1972: 82) but there is an important difference. The past-tense morpheme in USED TO can *only* correlate with past time reference, whereas WOULD is not thus restricted. The conditional element in WOULD is merely *compatible* with past time reference and in order for it to be able to bear a 'past habitual' interpretation, there must be a past time index present elsewhere in the utterance. Compare, for example:

119 I would mow the lawn.
120 I used to mow the lawn.

(120)—even out of context—refers to a habitual activity in the past, whereas (119) can do so only if we assume that a past time index such as 'when I was young' is somehow present in the context of utterance. (119) could just as easily correlate with a hypothetical index such as 'if you paid me'—so could (120) for that matter, but, significantly, there would still be a definite reference to past time and IF would tend to be interpreted as 'when'.

(114) is in many ways similar to (113), except that (114) would be spoken with an emphatic stress pattern and pitch contour. (114) could be paraphrased as:

114a   It was just typical of him to keep on all the time!

which is another way of describing disposition, at a time in the past, towards a given action. In this case, though, as well as the past time environment (the activity of 'keeping on' has presumably ceased at some time prior to the moment of utterance), WOULD also receives emphasis (hence JUST in the paraphrase) and so (114) is also something of an accusation.

Emphasis does not apply to WOULD only in its past time reference use. For example, if A has just bet B £5 that B will not jump into the swimming pool fully clothed, and B defiantly starts to walk towards the pool, A may well say something like:

121   My God, you would too!

Here, WOULD receives emphasis in a hypothetical conditioning environment.

There is not a great deal of difference between the use of WOULD in (115) and (116), since formality and politeness are often indistinguishable. Both are equivalent to WILL in the conditioning environment of 'formality/politeness'. (117) is also rather similar, and there the conditioning environment is a feeling of uncertainty on the part of the speaker. Finally, in (118) the conditioning environment is the past time reference of 'he said'.

It should be noted that the extremes of the six scales proposed above are by no means paraphrases of the possible pragmatic environments of the primary and secondary modals. Although the secondary modals certainly indicate more conditionality than the primary modals the difference is only relative, since the primary modals themselves are already a considerable distance from the leftmost extreme of the scale, since any element that can be described as 'modal' is necessarily to the right of an otherwise equivalent non-modal element. Note too that the leftmost extremes are defined negatively in terms of the rightmost extremes. This is because we are dealing with modal expressions and for our purposes the greater the degree of modality or conditionality of an expression, the more marked it is, whereas the less modal or conditional an expression, the less marked it is.

'Conditionality', therefore, turns out to be more or less the same thing as modality, and we can thus say that the secondary modals are more 'modal' than the primary modals. The specific notion of 'conditionality' used here, however, offers a more precise way of distinguishing between different degrees of modality in terms of the nature of particular conditioning environments which can be seen as manifestations of modality.

So far we have looked only at WOULD as the conditional counterpart of WILL, but similar observations can be made about the other secondary modals. Consider, for example, the following examples with COULD:

122 Last year I could still fit into my clothes. (past)
123 Could you tell me the right way to the market? (formal/polite)
124 Could Smith be the right man for the job? (tentative)
125 I could succeed, with the right financial backing. (hypothetical)
126 He said I could go. (indirect)

To take the last example first, if we consider (126) as a reported form of:

127 You can go.

the conditionality of COULD in (126) is due to the past time index contained in 'he said'. However, (126) could also be the reported form of:

128 You could go (if you wanted).

in which case the conditionality of COULD would be a result of the hypothetical condition shown in parentheses. A third possibility is that (127) could be reported as:

129 He said I can go.

—in other words, the permission is still in force. In this case the current relevance of the original deontic act overrides the significance of its being carried out in the past, and thus COULD is not necessary.

When the dynamic use of COULD correlates with past time reference as in (122), its meaning can be expressed as: 'circumstances were not such as to preclude X' last year. Note that it is not necessarily implied that the speaker actually did fit into his clothes (he may have been in bed in hospital, for example) as would have been the case had WAS ABLE TO been used (cf. Palmer, 1977: 5).

MIGHT is nearly always used as the conditional equivalent of MAY as a realization of epistemic modality, as in:

130 I might go if my cold's better. (hypothetical)

MIGHT in its epistemic sense cannot correlate with past time reference—cf.:

131 *When I was ten I might swim a mile.

There are, however, certain uses of MIGHT which can correlate with past time reference. For example:

132 Push as he might, the door still failed to open.
133 He said I might go. (i.e. 'permission' sense)

In (132), MIGHT is part of the (fairly productive) idiomatic structure 'V as NP might', and MIGHT is to be understood in its antiquated sense of 'physical power' (still preserved in the adjective MIGHTY and the noun MIGHT). In (133) when it is considered as the reported form of:

134 You may go.

MIGHT is the conditional equivalent of deontic MAY. (If it is the reported form of:

135 You might go.

it is epistemic.) In this deontic sense, however, MIGHT seems restricted to reported speech and to polite requests such as:

136 Might I have a light, please?

and is therefore less common than its epistemic counterpart.

SHOULD, which is fairly obviously the conditional counterpart of SHALL, and OUGHT TO, which, although etymologically distinct, is to all intents and purposes a conditional counterpart of MUST (although see below), can also have a limited past time deontic sense similar to MIGHT as in:

137 In my youth children did as they should/ought (to).

but usually they are used either in a non-past deontic sense, as in:

138 You should/ought to do as you're told.

or else in a dynamic/epistemic sense, as in:

139 That should/ought to be the postman now.

Thus in their most frequent uses, SHOULD and OUGHT TO (and MIGHT as well) can correlate with conditions of tentativeness/ hypothesis as in (138) and (139), and in addition they can also correlate with conditions of formality/politeness as in:

140 Should I help myself to another slice? (cf. 'Shall I')
141 Might I ask a favour of you? (cf. 'May I')
142 You oughtn't to pick your nose in public. (cf. 'mustn't')

SHOULD can occasionally occur as the conditional equivalent of dynamic/epistemic SHALL, with the same constraints on the person of the subject (cf. 3.3) as in:

143 If I were to fail my exams, should I be the only one?

although the less formal WOULD would probably be more usual here. SHOULD, however, also occurs without person restrictions in conditional clauses such as:

144 Should you happen to be passing, do drop in.

although in such cases there is no primary equivalent with SHALL. Here the SHOULD-clause appears to be a more formal/polite version of a corresponding version with IF. SHOULD is more commonly used, however, as a conditional equivalent of deontic SHALL, as in (138), although this is by no means clear cut, due to the fact that unlike deontic SHALL, with SHOULD the deontic source is not obviously the utterance which incorporates it, since:

145 You should go.

can only be reported as:

146 He said I should go.

or (significantly) as:

147 He said I ought to go.

and on this evidence SHOULD could just as easily be a conditional equivalent of deontic MUST. Conversely, OUGHT TO, while being the obvious contender for the conditional equivalent of MUST, could also be considered as a conditional equivalent of SHALL. One must conclude, therefore, that with the exception of the use of SHOULD in cases like (143) and (144), OUGHT TO and SHOULD are very similar as conditional equivalents of either SHALL or MUST. The similarity of SHOULD and OUGHT TO is evident in the following attested example spoken by a 12-year-old girl:

148 There ought to be a little window by there, shouldn't there?

(cf. also Poutsma, 1924: 75 and Palmer, 1979a: 100). This view of the overall closeness in meaning between SHOULD and OUGHT TO appears to be shared by most linguists (cf. for example, Anderson

(1971: 80), Ehrman (1966: 64), Halliday (1970a: 334), Leech (1971: 95), and Palmer (1974: 120)). One barely dissonant view is that of Close (1962: 119), who states that *'ought to* is generally felt to express a stronger sense of obligation than *should*; and it often replaces *should* when a more resounding word is felt to be necessary'. No arguments or evidence are given to support this claim, however.

In the light of the apparent invariance of the conditionality feature in the secondary modals, we can represent their core meanings as follows:

$$
\begin{array}{l}
\left.\begin{array}{l}\text{COULD}\\ \text{MIGHT}\end{array}\right\} : K(Z(C \text{ does not preclude } X))\\[1.2em]
\text{OUGHT TO} \;\; : K(Z(C \text{ entails } X))\\[0.8em]
\left.\begin{array}{l}\text{WOULD}\\ \text{SHOULD}\end{array}\right\} : K(Z(C \text{ is disposed towards } X))
\end{array}
$$

where Z = a condition. I have chosen to indicate the close relationship which exists between MUST and OUGHT TO by showing 'C entails X' to be part of the core meaning of both, although the difference between the representation of OUGHT TO as $K(Z(C$ entails $X))$ and that of SHOULD as $K(Z(C$ is disposed towards $X))$ is more apparent than real, since the imposing of conditions on 'C entails X' means that C on its own is effectively no more than simply disposed towards X.

The secondary modals, are to all intents and purposes, the same as their primary counterparts with regard to the extent to which they co-occur with negative particles (cf. Quirk *et al.*, 1972: 102 f.) and I will not go into any further detail here.

Notes

1. A much abridged and otherwise modified version of this chapter was published as Perkins (1982).
2. The syntactic features of the modals are well known and may be summarized as follows: (a) lack of −s in 3rd person singular; (b) absence of finite forms; (c) inability to co-occur with one another; (d) non-occurrence as the first element in imperatives; (e) always the first element of the verb phrase in which they occur. For more details see Palmer (1979a) and Coates (1983).
3. It should be recalled (cf. 2.4) that the term 'context' is being used here to refer to the linguistic environment of an expression (sometimes referred to as 'cotext') as well as to its non-linguistic environment (to which the term 'pragmatic' refers). Intonation, stress and other prosodic features may also be regarded as discrete contextual elements which influence the way in which an expression is to be interpreted, although I shall not have a great

deal to say about them in this book. For a description of modal usage which does take prosody into account to a greater extent, see Coates (1983).

4. Cf. Bouma (1975), Brown and Levinson (1978), Butler (1972), Calbert (1975), Cheng (1980), Lodge (1974), Pottier (1976), Seiler (1971), Simone and Amacker (1977), Shou-hsin (1980), Sohn (1974), Standwell (1979), and Steele (1975). I am grateful to Gwen Awbery, Magda Montgomery, and Larry Trask for information on Welsh, Polish, and Basque respectively.

5. See Kratzer (1977) for an analysis of CAN and MUST which is rather similar in spirit.

6. A similar observation with regard to the contextual specification of tense is made by O'Donnell (1977: 131) in his review of Palmer (1974).

7. MAY and MUST are being discussed together because although MAY resembles CAN in the way its component variables are related, it is far closer to MUST as regards the nature of the constraints upon the variables.

8. I am using 'entail' here slightly idiosyncratically: in strict logical parlance, entailment is a relationship between two (sets of) propositions p_1 and p_2 such that if p_1 is true, then p_2 is also true, although the reverse is not necessarily the case—e.g. if one knows that p_2, one cannot necessarily infer that p_1. However, if the formula for MUST is given a deontic reading the relationship of entailment holds not between two (sets of) propositions but between a deontic source and the occurrence of an event. It would be easy, of course, to stipulate that in such a case C represented the set of propositions which denoted the occurrence of the event, and some appropriate logical notation could then be used. In order to keep formal machinery to a minimum, however, I have used 'longhand' expressions like 'does not preclude that' (which could also be written as 'does not entail that not') and 'entails' which, although they are meant to apply with something like the rigour of more logically orthodox equivalents, are deliberately informal in order to enable the representation of direct relationships between laws, circumstances, and events, as well as between the propositional representations of such phenomena.

9. MAY thus has the same core meaning as CAN. This will be discussed shortly.

10. Despite the postulation of a common core meaning for MAY and CAN, it is worth pointing out that this account is, in fact, quite compatible with that of Coates (1980), who has argued for the non-equivalence of MAY and CAN. The non-equivalence which Coates describes is due (in my terms) to the different sets of constraints operating on the common core meaning.

11. Lightfoot (1974: 235) points out that such diachronic semantic changes are typical of the modals, and Anderson (1971: 83) similarly refers to many ' "shifts" that have occurred in the history of the English modals'.

12. Cf. Fitikides (1963: 107), Henderson (1945: 29), Opdycke (1946: 148, 508), Stratton (1940: 44), Treble and Vallins (1936: 40), and West and Kimber (1957: 117).

13. This distinction has also been noted by Coates (1983), Leech and Svartvik (1975: 143), Ney (1976: 14), and Quirk *et al.* (1972: 97).

14. Quirk *et al.* (1972: 385) say that epistemic MUSTN'T 'is not used at all', although Young (1980) notes that a sentence like 'We mustn't have come that way' would be quite acceptable in the dialect of Lancashire, and Lyons (1977: 801) too states that 'It mustn't be raining' uttered with the appropriate stress patterns' is equivalent to 'It can't be raining'. See also Hughes and Trudgill (1979: 23).

15. For something more along these lines see Coates (1983).
16. I shall from now on often use the terms epistemic, deontic, and dynamic as glosses for 'K = rational laws/C = evidence/X = the truth of p'; 'K = social laws/C = a deontic source/X = the occurrence of e'; 'K = natural laws/C = empirical cirumstances/X = the occurrence of e' respectively.
17. The scale of modal meaning ranging over possibility–probability–necessity and the way the meanings of the modals are distributed along such a scale has often been discussed (cf. Hermerén (1978) for a recent instance).
18. It is significant that they continue with the words: 'However, we didn't succeed in finding convincing evidence for this claim'.
19. Cf. the discussion of the relationship between the desiderative and the instrumental functions of language in 2.2.
20. In the corpus of spontaneous informal speech of children aged 6 to 12, to be discussed in 11.3, SHALL was used exclusively in first person interrogatives.
21. The fact that SHALL and WILL differ in markedness depending on the person of the subject was noted as early as 1765 by John Wallis (cf. Kemp, 1972: 339).
22. It is astonishing that grammars are still written in which it is maintained that 'it is incorrect, though increasingly common, to say *I will, we will* to express the future tense' (Phythian, 1980: 47).
23. The same phenomena have also been referred to as 'auxiliary vs. main verb negation' (Quirk *et al.*, 1972: 384), 'modality vs. thesis negation' (Halliday, 1970a: 332), and 'operator vs. nucleus negation' (Seuren, 1969 and Lee, 1975).
24. I.e. due to the cancelling out of negative operators in K(C does not not preclude X).
25. Anderson (1971: 76 f.) suggests a distinction which is roughly comparable, but his use of the term 'condition' is narrower and more traditional than mine. He regards COULD, for example, as containing a 'past' as well as a 'conditional' component, whereas in my formulation, as will be seen below, 'past' would merely be a particular instance of the more general feature 'conditional'.
26. The particle IF can perform a similar function to the so-called past-tense morpheme which differentiates the primary and secondary modals. For further discussion, see 9.2.

4 Quasi-Auxiliary Modal Expressions[1]

4.1 Introductory

In 2.2 the class of modal expressions was defined very roughly as that class of expressions which distinguishes non-categorical from categorical assertions, and Holmberg's (1979) category of A-indirectives from categorical directives. It has now further been established in Chapter 3 that the semantics of modal auxiliary verbs can be expressed as a relationship between a system of organized belief K, a set of circumstances C, the truth of a proposition p, or the occurrence of an event e, and, in the case of the secondary modals, a condition Z. It will be seen, in fact, that the core meanings of all modal expressions can be characterized as a relationship between, at most, these four variables, and such a relationship may thus be regarded as a semantic definition of 'modal expression'. It will be the principal aim of Chapters 4 to 8 to examine the way each modal expression differs with regard to the amount and type of information it expresses about these four variables, and with regard to the way it relates them. I will also examine certain types of formal entity with which each modal expression may co-occur—i.e. that which makes a syntactic characterization possible—and this will often be seen to be related to the type of meaning each expression can be used to express. However, the grammatical information included is not intended to be exhaustive and is only included if, and in so far as, it appears to throw light upon distinguishing semantic characteristics, and, occasionally, if it is thought to be of independent interest.

I have organized Chapters 4 to 7 largely according to syntactic criteria, but further subdivisions, sometimes on non-syntactic grounds, are often needed, and there are a few rather idiosyncratic modal expressions which are not entirely at home in the category allotted to them on formal grounds. This is because the overall pattern to which modal expressions may be seen to conform is rather complex, and any treatment which failed to do justice to this fact would inevitably turn out to be over-simplistic. A summary of the most prominent distinguishing features of each category of modal expressions will be included in Chapter 8.

It should be noted, finally, that it has not been my intention to include every single modal expression in English, although the choice of modal expressions covered is intended to be fairly representative of the full range available.

4.2 HAVE(GOT)TO[2]

The meaning of HAVE(GOT)TO can best be distinguished by comparing it with that of MUST. Leech (1969: 227 f.) reasonably suggests that:

149 You must be in camp by ten.

'would probably be spoken by an officer giving orders', whereas:

150 You have to be in camp by ten.

'could well be spoken by an ordinary soldier informing his comrades of orders issued by someone else'. Antinucci and Parisi (1971: 35), who also cite Leech's example, add that 'Must seems to imply that the speaker puts his authority, as it were, into the causing event, while this is not the case with have to'. (Cf. also Larkin, 1976: 392.) Palmer (1979c: 189) quite categorically states that HAVE TO and HAVE GOT TO 'clearly deny the speaker's involvement'. However, given that Palmer does not distinguish between core meaning and contextual meaning, his statement is problematical in that the 'lack of speaker's involvement' expressed by HAVE(GOT)TO may be overridden by the pragmatic component of an utterance. For example, HAVE(GOT)TO constitutes a more 'impersonal' version of MUST and will often be used in situations where a degree of politeness or formality is required, and where MUST might appear too intrusive and direct, but this is not to deny that it may be clear from the context of utterance that it is the speaker's authority alone that is in question. The essential point to note is that whereas the *core* meaning of MUST is compatible with a deontic source which may or may not be the speaker, the *core* meaning of HAVE(GOT)TO is compatible only with a deontic source which is external to the speaker. But if one does not make a distinction between some kind of core meaning and some kind of contextual meaning, it is not possible to show how HAVE(GOT)TO can deny the speaker's involvement.

Coates (1983: 4.3) feels that non-epistemic HAVE TO expresses objective modality, whereas non-epistemic HAVE GOT TO is subjective; but although the corpus examples cited by Coates do reveal that use of HAVE GOT TO *tends* to indicate greater speaker involvement than use of HAVE TO, the deontic source representing the C variable still remains explicitly objective—i.e. outside the speaker's control.

In addition to expressing objective deontic modality, HAVE(GOT)TO is also used on occasion to express dynamic modality, as in:

151 We have to wait another six months for the harvest.

—i.e. the C variable refers to empirical circumstances—and in addition may be used, though far less commonly in British than American English, to express epistemic modality—i.e. the C variable refers to evidence (cf. Palmer, 1979a: 46). The following sentence, for example, would not be unusual in American English:

152 This has to be the biggest ant-hill ever seen.

If MUST is substituted for HAVE TO in (152) the forcefulness of the sentence appears to be reduced (cf. Leech, 1971: 77), which can be accounted for on the grounds that HAVE(GOT)TO expresses *objective* epistemic modality. In other words, the conclusiveness of the evidence on the basis of which the speaker makes his claim is dependent upon circumstances over which the speaker has no control. MUST, on the other hand, appears to be compatible with either objective or subjective epistemic modality—the latter being a case where the conclusiveness of the evidence is arrived at via the speaker's own mental deductive processes, which are his own subjective province. I shall have more to say about objective modality below (especially in 5.1), but it is worth pointing out here that the distinction between MUST and HAVE(GOT)TO in terms of objectivity/subjectivity also distinguishes the class of modal auxiliaries from most other modal expressions.[3]

Since the same 'objectivity' appears to be present whether HAVE(GOT)TO expresses dynamic or epistemic modality,[4] it seems safe to assume that it is part of the core meaning of HAVE(GOT)TO which can therefore be represented as K(C entails X), where: (i) K = social laws/C = a deontic source (most typically);[5] (ii) C is external to the speaker's control; (iii) C is external to the subject.[6]

HAVE(GOT)TO and MUST also differ distributionally in that with MUST a negative operator always negates the proposition/event (cf. 3.3.4), whereas with HAVE(GOT)TO it is nearly always the modality which is negated, as in:

153 You don't have to/haven't got to[7] thank me.

However, occasionally HAVEN'T GOT TO and DON'T HAVE TO,

when used to express deontic modality, appear to negate the event, as in:

154 You haven't got to park on double yellow lines—it's against the law.

which appears to express prohibition, rather than a lack of obligation (cf. Palmer, 1979a: 95 f.).

Unlike MUST, HAVE(GOT)TO has both past and non-past tense forms and can co-occur with auxiliary verbs in the same verb phrase.

4.3 NEED TO

NEED TO differs semantically from both MUST and HAVE(GOT)TO in the following way. We have seen that MUST by itself gives no clue as to the identity or nature of a deontic source or empirical circumstance, apart from the fact that it is such as to entail the occurrence of a given event. HAVE(GOT)TO is more specific in that it excludes (if only directly) the speaker from being the deontic source/empirical circumstance. If I 'have to' rest, there is no requirement that I be personally responsible for such a state of affairs which would normally be due to some set of circumstances not seen as originating in my own decision. If a chair 'has got to' be reupholstered, or a watch 'has to' be wound, it is because some external authority or circumstance has compelled that this is what must happen. HAVE(GOT)TO thus indicates that compulsion is, or has been, imposed from without. NEED TO is more explicit than MUST in a slightly different way. It indicates a compulsion which comes from *within*. If I 'need to' rest, I feel a compulsion which, although it may be non-personal and beyond my control, is still felt to originate within myself. Similarly, if we speak of a chair that 'needs to' be repaired or a watch that 'needs to' be wound, we are referring to states which we see as originating in, or as being properties of, a particular chair or a particular watch. However, although such compulsions are seen to originate within, and in some cases where the subject of the sentence is in the first person are seen to originate within the speaker himself, they are still explicitly objective, as is the case with HAVE(GOT)TO, since they come from a part of the speaker over which he has no conscious control. If I 'need to' drink, it is because I cannot control my thirst. If I 'need to' make a new start in life, it is because something within me rebels against the way of life I am currently leading.[8]

As is the case with HAVE(GOT)TO, the core meaning of NEED TO denies the speaker's involvement, although it may sometimes be used in an utterance which has the overall illocutionary force of a directive, in which case the directive element, which is ultimately due to the speaker's wishes, must always be supplied by the cotext of NEED TO or by the context of utterance. For example, if:

155 You need to get your hair cut.

were addressed by a sergeant-major to a private, it would no doubt be understood as an order, but this would be due to the difference in role and status between the sergeant-major and the private and also the circumstances in which it was uttered, rather than to the core meaning of NEED TO. It is possible, therefore, to represent the core meaning of NEED TO as K(C entails X), where: (i) K = natural laws/C = empirical circumstances (typically); (ii) C is external to the speaker's control; (iii) C is internal to the subject.

Like the modal auxiliary NEED, NEED TO when used with a negative particle is itself negated as opposed to the event.

The non-tautologous nature of a sentence like:

156 You needn't go to the toilet if you don't need to.

clearly brings out the difference between auxiliary NEED and non-auxiliary NEED TO, which closely parallels the distinction between auxiliary MUST and non-auxiliary HAVE TO. It is that whereas auxiliary NEED is compatible with either a subjective or an objective interpretation, NEED TO is restricted to an objective interpretation. A further parallel is that NEED TO (and its past tense form NEEDED TO) can co-occur with auxiliaries in the same verb phrase and with the same range of tense and aspectual forms as HAVE(GOT)TO, unlike the more restricted NEED and MUST.

4.4 HAD BETTER

HAD BETTER can be used only to express deontic modality, and it is objective in that the deontic source is not (directly) identifiable as the speaker. With HAD BETTER there is the further explicit information that, in the speaker's view, it is 'better' that the event be brought about than that it not be brought about, in view of the adverse consequences in the latter case (cf. Palmer, 1979a: 69). Cf., for example:

157 We'd better dress up warmly.

There is, furthermore, a conditional element included in the meaning of HAD BETTER (realized in the past tense form HAD) and it is thus similar in meaning to SHOULD and OUGHT TO when used to express conditional deontic modality. In all other non-auxiliary modal expressions, conditionality can be expressed by the use of WOULD.

The core meaning of HAD BETTER can thus be shown as K(Z(C entails X)), where (i) K = social laws/C = a deontic source; (ii) C is external to the speaker's control; (iii) C is external to the subject; (iv) C is such that not-X entails adverse consequences.

When HAD BETTER is accompanied by a negative particle, it is always the event which is negated, as in:

158 We'd better not do it too high.
159 You hadn't better go.

HAD BETTER is similar to the modal auxiliaries as regards the aspectual forms with which it may co-occur, and despite its deontic meaning it co-occurs with them quite freely, as in:

160 I'd better be going now.
161 You'd better be studying hard for your exams.
162 He'd better have done a good job on the car.
163 You'd better have been keeping up to date on policy changes.

4.5 Quasi modal auxiliaries compared with modal auxiliaries

After looking at no more than three non-auxiliary modal expressions, a clear picture is already beginning to emerge regarding the way they differ from the modal auxiliaries. Although the non-auxiliaries express a relationship between (some of) the variables K, C, X, and Z, they differ from the auxiliaries in that they incorporate more circumstantial information in their core meanings—i.e. they are more *explicit* about the nature and identity of C. Compared with the non-auxiliary modal expressions—and this will prove to be true of all non-auxiliary modal expressions —the modal auxiliaries are more vague as to the identity and nature of the C variable, and thus more inexplicit as indicators of what type of modality is being expressed by the utterance in which they are used. This observation about the nature of the modal auxiliaries will be amply borne out in Chapters 5 to 8.

Notes

1. I have grouped together under one heading the three modal expressions to be dealt with in this chapter on the grounds that they are fairly close in meaning to certain modal auxiliaries, and do not fit into any of the other categories to be proposed.

2. For present purposes I am not distinguishing between HAVE TO and HAVE GOT TO, as their core meanings are very nearly identical—the major semantic distinction being that HAVE TO can have habitual aspect, whereas HAVE GOT TO cannot. Other distinctions are largely pragmatic (e.g. HAVE GOT TO is more informal) or grammatical (HAVE GOT TO has no non-finite forms). For more extensive discussion of the differences see Haegeman (1980) and Coates (1983), bearing in mind the reservation in 4.2 below.

3. Cf. Young (1980), who notes that 'where there is a straight contrast between modal verbs and non-modal verbs [i.e. non-auxiliary modal verbs] the modal ones are subjective and the non-modal objective'.

4. As is the case with many other modal expressions, with HAVE(GOT)TO it is sometimes not clear, even in context, whether an epistemic or a dynamic sense is intended, as is the case in the following extract from the *Guardian* (August 31st, 1979, p. 13): 'But as he surveys the Arab world today, and compares it with what, according to his predictions and calculations, it should have been, he *has to* concede that they have gone hopelessly awry.' It is not clear here whether we have to do with conclusive evidence for truth or with sufficient empirical circumstances.

5. Here, and below, I will merely state the type of modality which the expression in question is primarily, or most typically, used to express. It will be clear from the discussion here and in Chapter 3 that it is rarely, if ever, possible to say that a given expression can express *only* this type of modality or can never express that type of modality. Virtually all modal expressions are comparatively flexible with regard to the way their relativity may shift from one set of laws to another.

6. The reason for (iii) will be made clear in 4.3.

7. HAVEN'T TO is possible in some dialects—cf. Leech (1971: 87).

8. The distinctions described in this paragraph do not appear to have been appreciated in even the more recent discussions of the modals—e.g. Coates (1983) and Haegeman (1981).

5 Adjectival, Participial, and Nominal Modal Expressions

5.1 TO, THAT, and BE

Leech (1971: 107 ff.), in his discussion of 'factual' vs. 'theoretical' meaning, points out that complements consisting of a THAT-clause or a gerund construction are generally concerned with facts (i.e. factual meaning), whereas complements consisting of infinitive constructions are, more often than not, concerned with ideas (i.e. theoretical meaning). A similar conclusion is reached by Kiparsky and Kiparsky (1970), who provide evidence that factive complements (i.e. complements in which the truth of the propositional content is presupposed by the speaker) cannot be infinitival,[1] whereas THAT-clauses may be either factive or non-factive. (Earlier transformational accounts of complement constructions, e.g. Rosenbaum (1967), assumed that gerunds, infinitives, and THAT-clauses were all derived from the same type of deep structure and that they were therefore semantically equivalent.)

The relevance of such observations to the present discussion is that although many modal expressions can take infinitival, gerundive, or THAT-complements, there are a considerable number which can take only an infinitival *or* a THAT-complement, and a few that can take only a gerundive complement. Significantly, those modal expressions (whether they be verbal, adverbial, adjectival, or nominal) which are restricted to infinitival or gerundive complements nearly always express either deontic or dynamic modality, which are both concerned with the occurrence of non-actual events. Furthermore, lexical items like POSSIBILITY which *can* occur with THAT-complements generally express deontic or dynamic modality when they take an infinitival or a gerundive complement. A possible explanation for why this should be so is suggested by a consideration of the difference in meaning between THAT and TO.

The use of THAT as a conjunction or a 'complementizer' is a development from its original deictic use as a demonstrative pronoun, and may be seen as a means of signalling that the clause which follows it—i.e. the complement—differs in status from that which preceeds it—i.e. the main clause. It is merely an ostensive device, however, and places no restrictions on the factivity of the complement. Hence both the following are possible:

164 I am amazed that you're here. (factive)
165 I am convinced that you're here. (non-factive)

The infinitival particle TO, however, is very different in its origins. Its many uses appear to derive from an original use as a preposition to express 'a spatial or local relation' or 'motion directed towards and reaching' (*Shorter O.E.D.*: 2315), from which have developed secondary meanings such as 'purpose', 'result', and 'specification of a future point in time'. The tendency of forms which express spatial relations to develop meanings which are related only analogically to spatial relations has been exploited by proponents of the lexicalist hypothesis, and it is well known that in many languages besides the better-known European ones, expressions which refer to motion or location also refer to temporal relations. In Coptic, for example, the preposition 'E', meaning 'toward', is also used to indicate future time (Fries, 1927: 91), and in some Indonesian languages the future preverb was originally a preposition meaning 'to, towards' (Ultan, 1972). It seems reasonable to assume, therefore, that the use of TO in English often described in terms of 'purpose' or 'intention', and the non-factivity of infinitival complements, are attributable to a more fundamental meaning of TO which could be described as signalling a state or event which is unattained or unrealized at a point in time which would normally be specified by the tense of the preceding main verb.

The presence of the verb BE[2] in a great many English modal expressions is also highly significant. To predicate a state of affairs by using the verb BE is to assert that state of affairs categorically; thus when BE is used in a modal expression, it categorically asserts the modality expressed. Compare the following, for example:

166 He may be mad.
167 It *is* possible that he's mad.

Both (166) and (167) could be said to express some kind of possibility, but whereas in (166) the possibility might merely be a figment of the speaker's own imagination, in (167) it is referred to as actually existing independently of the speaker. In (166) the possibility is merely expressed, but in (167) it is categorically asserted, since the possibility is presumably based on unquestioned evidence. As support for this, consider the view expressed by Lyons (1977: 805 f.), who notes that conditional clauses are incompatible with subjective espistemic modal expressions and argues that a sentence like:

168 If it may rain, you should take your umbrella.

is acceptable only if it is taken as expressing objective epistemic modality as opposed to subjective epistemic modality. The following:

169 If it is possible that it will rain, you should take your umbrella.

on the other hand, is far more natural, since there is little doubt that objective epistemic modality is being expressed.

The view taken here is that all modal expressions which incorporate the verb BE express objective modality, the objectivity being a function of the fact that the modality itself is actually asserted. This helps to explain why COULD in:

170 Ali could defeat anyone he fought with when he was twenty-five.

does not reveal whether or not Ali actually *did* defeat everyone he fought with, whereas WAS ABLE TO in:

171 Ali was able to defeat anyone he fought with when he was twenty-five.

actually implies that he did defeat them. COULD in (170) merely expresses the nature of Ali's ability at the age of twenty-five, whereas WAS ABLE TO in (171) claims that the ability was actually realized.[3] That this is due to WAS, rather than to any inherent meaning of ABLE,[4] can be seen by comparing (171) with:

172 Ali $\begin{cases} \text{seemed} \\ \text{looked} \\ \text{felt} \end{cases}$ able to defeat anyone he fought with when he was twenty-five.

All the modal auxiliaries are compatible with either a subjective or an objective interpretation (depending on the context of course), whereas the vast majority of non-auxiliary modal expressions— especially those containing BE—are inherently objective.[5]

This difference is also apparent in the fact that the modal auxiliaries are far more integrated within the structure of the clause they qualify than most of the non-auxiliary modal expressions which, in the case of those which incorporate BE or a main verb, virtually constitute their own separate clause.

5.2 IS TO

In the light of the above discussion of BE and TO, it is relatively easy to account for the meaning of IS TO. Literally, IS TO states that circumstances which currently exist are disposed towards the occurrence of an event which is as yet unrealized.[6] Besides this literal meaning, IS TO implies that the circumstances in question are due to some conscious organization. This can be seen in the fact that one does not, under normal circumstances, say:

173 The sun is to rise tomorrow morning. (?)

for how could the rising of the sun be consciously organized? Compare (173) with:

174 The sun will rise tomorrow morning.

which does not presuppose any conscious organization. (174) merely states that circumstances are disposed towards the rising of the sun tomorrow morning. (173) becomes acceptable, however, if we regard it as being uttered by some omnipotent being who *is* capable of consciously organizing such things.

While the source of such conscious organization is often human, as in:

175 You are to take these four times daily.

or at least animate, as in the 'omnipotent' reading of (173), this does not have to be the case. Sometimes the laws of reason themselves may be regarded as the source of the disposition, as in:

176 Such an outcome is to be expected.

and sometimes the world-view presupposed by IS TO is not always entirely accurate regarding the extent to which circumstances are actually disposed towards the envisaged event, as in:

177 You are not to bully your playmates, Igor.

Leech (1971: 96) feels that the 'principal meaning [of IS TO] includes the specific idea of "ordering" or "commanding" ', but this would appear to be a function of the context rather than of the core meaning of IS TO. For example, although:

178 You are to marry him within the next six months.

if spoken by a father to a daughter he wanted to get married off, would certainly be interpreted as a command, if it were uttered by a fortune-teller during a session with one of her clients, it would normally be regarded as meaning that the 'stars' are so disposed.

IS TO is sometimes regarded as denoting future time reference (e.g. by Palmer, 1979a: 146), but although this is certainly true, it appears to be an incidental, rather than a central, feature of its meaning, since any event which, in real time, occurs partially as a result of circumstances which are disposed towards it cannot but occur after them. Palmer's example of IS TO used as a 'pure' future—namely:

179 McKenzie's figures now two for twenty-three—he's to bowl to Parfitt.

and his example of IS TO used as a ' "pure" future in the past'—namely:

180 Worse was to follow.

are clear evidence of this.

IS TO does, in fact, have much in common with WILL, which has often been regarded as a future tense morpheme (cf. 3.3.3), but they differ in that with IS TO the C variable is objective and (usually) consciously organized. The core meaning of IS TO can thus be represented as K(C is disposed towards X), where: (i) K = natural laws/C = empirical circumstances (typically); (ii) C is objective; (iii) C is consciously organized (typically).

When IS TO co-occurs with NOT or N'T in an utterance which expresses dynamic modality, it appears to be the modality which is negated, whereas if the utterance expresses deontic modality, the event is typically negated (cf. Palmer, 1979a: 147); thus in:

181 You aren't to marry him, and that's an order!

the event is negated, whereas in:

182 You aren't to marry him, as I read it in the cards.

the modality appears to be negated, although it is difficult to find conclusive evidence for such judgements (cf. the discussion in 3.3.4).

Unlike HAVE TO and NEED TO, but like the modal auxiliaries, IS TO cannot co-occur with a modal auxiliary in the same verb phrase, and the only common tense-aspect combination with IS TO is between past tense and perfective aspect, as in:

183 She was to have come by train.

5.3 Expressions incorporating only BE . . . TO

This category of expressions is further defined by the fact that the item in the BE . . . TO frame cannot be used attributively or pre-dicatively, or, in the case of APT, not with the same sense.

5.3.1 BE GOING TO

BE GOING TO consists essentially of the meaning of IS and TO together with that of GOING, which relates the occurrence of the event expressed in the infinitival complement to a currently existing process or state of affairs which is seen by the speaker as being instrumental in bringing about the event. Its core meaning can be represented as K(C is disposed towards X), where: (i) K = natural laws/C = empirical circumstances (typically); (ii) C is objective; (iii) C involves a current ongoing process.

One of the most common secondary uses of BE GOING TO is to refer to the future, and it is thus an example of what Ultan (1972) refers to as an 'andative' future—namely an expression which incorporates an item originally used to express motion away from the speaker, but which has developed the additional meaning of temporal progression away from the present moment (cf. also Halpern, 1975). Andative futures are apparently one of the most common types of linguistic device used for referring to future time in languages throughout the world (cf. Jespersen, 1924: 260 f.) and the combination of GOING with TO results in an expression which is thus doubly apt for the expression of future time.

BE GOING TO has often been regarded as a near synonym of WILL with regard to the expression of future time, and there are certainly occasions when it is apparently of little concern which of the two expressions one uses, as in the following attested example:

184 We're going to start (treating?) things now, won't we?

There are, however, a number of important differences between them. One of the clearest and best-known summaries of these differences is that of Binnick (1971, 1972), although much of what he has to say can also be found in McIntosh (1966). However, although Binnick makes a number of interesting observations, he can offer no single explanation for them. Palmer (1979a: 120 ff.) too, in a fairly full discussion of BE GOING TO, does little more than describe its various uses and adds little that is new. However, if the meanings of WILL and BE GOING TO are analysed in the way that has been suggested above, it is possible to account fairly systematically for the various ways in which they differ, as noted by Binnick and others.

Binnick begins his second article (1972: 3) with the general statement: 'A sentence containing *will* which refers to the future is often felt to be "elliptical" in the sense that the sentence is incomplete as it stands, some part of it being "understood" ', whereas 'sentences with the *be going to* future are never felt to be elliptical'. He compares the following two sentences:

185 The rock'll fall.
186 The rock is going to fall.

saying that one feels that (185), as it stands, seems in need of completion by some such clause as 'if you pull the wedge out from under it', whereas (186) does not. No satisfactory explanation is given.

In the analysis of WILL proposed in 3.3.3, it was shown that the meaning of WILL can be expressed as 'circumstances are disposed towards the occurrence of an event e', with no further information regarding the actual nature of the circumstances. With BE GOING TO, on the other hand, the circumstances pertinent to the occurrence of the event in question are clearly identified as involving a current ongoing process which will ultimately lead to the occurrence of the event. Thus whereas in (186) the falling of the rock is shown to be the result of an ongoing process of which the outcome is virtually preordained, in (185) the falling of the rock is expressed simply as a general disposition which, by itself, is insufficient actually to bring about the event.

More specific consequences of Binnick's notion of ellipsis are exemplified in:

187 I'll kill Sam if you ask me to.
188 I'm going to kill Sam if you ask me to. (?)

He points out (1971: 42) that here WILL is preferable to BE GOING TO with IF- and UNLESS-clauses, and that (188) is rather strange. Here again, the fact that with BE GOING TO the circumstances are regarded as virtually sufficient to bring about the event means that they are unconditional, whereas the disposition expressed by WILL is insufficient by itself to bring about the event and any further conditional requirements must be indicated elsewhere.

5.3.2 *BE ABOUT TO*

BE ABOUT TO resembles BE GOING TO in that it is used to refer to future time and incorporates an item originally used to refer to spatial relationships. The distinguishing characteristic of BE ABOUT TO, however, is that the event referred to is regarded as imminent (cf. the spatial sense of ABOUT—namely, 'in the (immediate) vicinity'). Its core meaning can therefore be represented as K(C is disposed towards X), where: (i) K = natural laws/C = empirical circumstances; (ii) C is objective; (iii) C is such that X seems imminent.

BE ABOUT TO also differs from BE GOING TO in that it does not comfortably co-occur with the progressive aspect—cf.:

189 The plane is about to take off.
190 The plane is about to be taking off. (?)

5.3.3 BE BOUND TO

BE BOUND TO differs from the other expressions in this group in that it is most frequently used to express epistemic modality, as in:

191 He's bound to win—no one else can touch him.

(cf. Palmer, 1979a: 45), although it may sometimes be used to express deontic modality, as in:

192 You are bound by law to wear a seat belt.

In its compatibility with both epistemic and deontic modality, BE BOUND TO resembles HAVE(GOT)TO, except that whereas BE BOUND TO is more commonly used in an epistemic sense, HAVE(GOT)TO is more frequent in its deontic sense. BE BOUND TO also resembles HAVE(GOT)TO in incorporating the notion of compulsion, but with BE BOUND TO the compulsion is such that— at least when used epistemically—the referent of the X variable is regarded as inevitable. The core meaning of BE BOUND TO can thus be represented as K(C entails X), where: (i) K = rational laws/C = evidence (typically); (ii) C is objective; (iii) C is such that X is inevitable.

When used deontically, BE BOUND TO can have two distinct negative meanings, depending on the position of the negative particle, as can be seen in:

193 You're not bound by law to beat your wife.

i.e. wife-beating is not compulsory, and:

194 You're bound by law not to beat your wife.

—i.e. wife-beating is illegal. When used to express epistemic modality, on the other hand, BE BOUND TO typically has only one negative meaning, as in:

195 He's bound not to win.

Examples like:

196 He's not bound to win.

are possible, but would normally be used only to contradict a sentence like (195), or in circumstances where 'he's bound to win' were contextually explicit.

5.3.4 BE LIABLE TO and BE APT TO

BE LIABLE TO and BE APT TO have rather similiar meanings. BE LIABLE TO incorporates the specific connotation that the event is not entirely wished for—cf.:

197 He's liable to break a leg if he carries on like that.

An example like:

198 You're liable to have a good time if you're not careful.

could be used only ironically. This connotation derives from the original, and still occasionally used, sense of LIABLE which refers to being subjected to, or being bound by, some system of social laws. In its current sense, however, the laws involved are natural rather than social. The core meaning of BE LIABLE TO can be expressed as K(C is disposed towards X), where: (i) K = natural laws/C = empirical circumstances (typically); (ii) C is objective; (iii) C is such that X is unsolicited and not entirely wished for.

BE APT TO, on the other hand, carries the implication that the circumstances which are disposed towards X involve the tendency of such an event to occur on previous occasions—cf.:

199 He's apt to get excited.

The core meaning of BE APT TO can thus be represented as K(C is disposed towards X), where: (i) K = natural laws/C = empirical circumstances; (ii) C is objective; (iii) C involves the previous tendency of X to occur.

It should be noted that when APT occurs in the frame IT BE . . . THAT, it refers to the *suitability* of a state of affairs which is seen as actual, as in:

200 It's rather apt that you have been chosen.

or of which the future actuality is already preordained, as in:

201 It's rather apt that you should be going to Peru.

and as such is used to express evaluative modality, with which we are not concerned in this book (cf. 2.1).

5.3.5 BE ABLE TO and BE WILLING TO

BE ABLE TO and BE WILLING TO, together with their negative versions BE UNABLE TO and BE WILLING TO, differ from the other modal expressions in 5.3 in that what they predicate is regarded as a disposition of the subject of the sentence, and, furthermore, a property of an animate being. Although the latter condition may appear to be violated in an example like:

202 This chair is able to be repaired.

this is not quite the case, since when BE ABLE TO is used in this way, the referent of the subject almost seems to take on an anthropomorphic quality.

In Palmer's (1974: 100 ff. and elsewhere) terminology both BE ABLE TO and BE WILLING TO are subject oriented (cf. 3.3.2).

BE ABLE TO is often regarded as a near paraphrase—if not a synonym—of CAN in certain uses of the latter, but a number of differences can be noted. Palmer (1979a: 76 f.) isolates four principal 'conditions that favour the use of BE ABLE TO rather than CAN' which, roughly, are:

a. CAN has no non-finite forms and BE ABLE TO thus serves as a suppletive form.
b. BE ABLE TO is only equivalent in meaning to CAN used in its 'ability' sense.
c. BE ABLE TO is more formal than CAN.
d. BE ABLE TO is often used to indicate 'actuality': IS ABLE TO = 'can and does'; whereas CAN is not used in this way: CAN = 'can and will do'.

These observations merit further discussion and some can be explained by means of the present framework of analysis.

(a) is evident in the fact that in the corpus of spontaneous speech of 6–12-year-old children discussed in 11.3, CAN was used 473 times, whereas BE ABLE TO was used only 6 times and on every occasion was used together with an auxiliary verb in a sense which would have been impossible or inexplicit with CAN alone.(Cf. 11.3, where the actual examples are given.)[7] (c) also finds some confirmation here in that the entire corpus was recorded in an informal situation with no adult present.

With regard to (b) it appears certain, at least according to the analysis being proposed here, that CAN and BE ABLE TO themselves are *never* exact synonyms, although the parallel between the meaning of a given sentence containing CAN and that of another sentence containing BE ABLE TO may well be extremely close. In BE ABLE TO the notion of ability has been objectified. CAN, on the other hand, is neutral with regard to objectivity/subjectivity and expresses nothing more than a relation of 'non-preclusion' between a set of circumstances and an event. Although we may infer the notion of ability from such a relationship, such an inference would itself constitute a kind of objectification process, attributing objectivity to a part of the linguistic system where none, in fact, exists. The objectified notion of ability is easy to manipulate—both conceptually and linguistically—whereas the notion of 'can' is extremely difficult to discuss unless one objectifies it into notions like ability, possibility, potentiality, etc.

Palmer's fourth condition can similarly be explained in terms of the objectivity of BE ABLE TO, as was shown in 5.1 above.

The core meaning of BE ABLE TO may be represented as K(C does not preclude X), where: (i) K = natural laws/C = empirical circumstances; (ii) C is objective; (iii) C involves a property inherent in the subject of the sentence.

Mention should perhaps be made here of BE CAPABLE OF, which is similar in meaning to BE ABLE TO, except that whereas BE ABLE TO can sometimes imply previous actuality, BE CAPABLE OF never can.

The core meaning of BE WILLING TO may be represented as K(C is disposed towards X), where K = psychological laws/C = a property of human consciousness; (ii) C is objective. This is our first example so far of an expression which is used solely to express boulomaic modality (cf. 2.1).

WILL, in some of its uses, and BE WILLING TO are often regarded as synonyms in the same way as CAN and BE ABLE TO, but they too may be distinguished on similar grounds—namely:

 (i) WILL has no finite forms and BE WILLING TO thus serves as a suppletive form.
 (ii) BE WILLING TO is only equivalent to WILL used in 'volitional' contexts—i.e. with BE WILLING TO the notion of volition is made explicit, whereas with WILL it is not.
(iii) BE WILLING TO is often more formal than WILL.

With regard to (i) and (iii) it is significant that in the corpus of child language referred to above, WILL was used 420 times, whereas BE WILLING TO was not used at all.

Besides taking an infinitival complement, BE WILLING TO can also occasionally occur with a THAT-complement, as in:

203 I am willing that you should go.

and it is thus slightly idiosyncratic within the present group, where it has been included on account of its affinities with BE ABLE TO.

5.4 Expressions incorporating non-verbally-derived adjectives

This category is restricted to modal expressions which incorporate an adjective which is not clearly a productive combination of verb root plus suffix (as is largely the case with the expressions included in 5.5) although this may, in fact, be the case historically. In addition, every adjective in this class as well as being used predicatively may also be used attributively with a similar modal meaning. A further characteristic is that they can all be used impersonally with an IT-subject.

5.4.1 BE SURE TO/THAT, BE CERTAIN TO/THAT, BE LIKELY TO/THAT[8]

The core meanings of these three expressions can be represented as follows: BE SURE TO/THAT: K(C entails X), where: (i) K = rational laws/C = evidence; (ii) C is objective; (iii) C involves 'sureness'. BE CERTAIN TO/THAT: K(C entails X), where: (i) K = rational laws/C = evidence; (ii) C is objective; (iii) C involves 'certainty'. BE LIKELY TO/THAT: K(C is disposed towards X), where: (i) K = rational laws/C = evidence; (ii) C is objective; (iii) C involves 'likelihood'.

The characterization of C in the above as involving 'sureness', 'certainty', and 'likelihood' respectively indicates that the individuating properties of each expression are in large part due to the nature of the lexical items SURE, CERTAIN, and LIKELY. Given the limitations of this book, it will not normally be feasible to offer an analysis of such lexical items, apart from indicating the type of modality they most typically express.

When used with TO, the subject of BE SURE, BE CERTAIN, and BE LIKELY is always the same as that of the infinitival complement, as is evident in:

204 They're sure to come.
205 He's certain to fall at the first fence.
206 He's likely to inherit millions.

A greater range of meanings is possible when they are used with a THAT-complement. For example, with BE SURE THAT and BE CERTAIN THAT the subject of the main clause does not have to be the same as that of the complement—cf.:

207 I'm sure that he'll come.
208 They're certain that she's run away.

BE LIKELY THAT differs, however, in that it can occur only with an impersonal IT-subject—cf.:

209 It's likely that we're done for.
210 *We're likely that we're done for.

which is no doubt connected with the fact that likelihood is not a mental state like sureness and certainty, but is empirically determined.

Another difference between THAT-complements and infinitival complements which is relevant here—and this is true of all modal expressions which can take both—is that the former allows for greater variety and complexity as regards tense and co-occurrence with other sentential elements—cf.:

211 I'm sure that $\begin{cases} \text{he will come.} \\ \text{he had come.} \\ \text{he might possibly have been about to come.} \end{cases}$

whereas the latter consists of an unmarked verb and, at most if at all, an adverb or adverbial clause or phrase.

BE LIKELY TO/THAT is further differentiated from both BE SURE TO/THAT and BE CERTAIN TO/THAT in that when it occurs with a negative particle—whether it comes before LIKELY or in the complement clause—it is always the complement clause which is negated—cf.:

He's not likely to come. = He's likely not to come.
It's not likely that he'll come. = It's likely that he won't come.

This phenomenon has been variously described as 'transferred negation' (e.g. Quirk *et al.*, 1972: 789 f.), 'negative raising' (e.g. Stockwell *et al.*, 1973: 253 ff.), and 'negative transportation' (e.g. Lakoff, 1969), and is a feature of several other modal expressions, as we shall see (cf. also 3.3.4). In contrast, with BE SURE TO/THAT and BE CERTAIN TO/THAT, when the negative particle occurs in the main clause it is the modality which is negated—cf.:

He's not sure/certain to come. ≠ He's sure/certain not to come.
It's not sure/certain that he'll come. ≠ It's sure/certain that he won't come.

Compare also:

He's not likely not to come. = He's likely to come.
He's not sure/certain not to come. ≠ He's sure/certain to come.

Sheintuch and Wise (1976) have suggested that whether or not an expression is subject to transferred negation is due to pragmatic factors. Briefly, if the expression indicates either (a) uncertainty on the part of the speaker (e.g. BELIEVE, THINK, IMAGINE), (b) lack of control on the part of the matrix subject over the state of affairs in the complement clause (e.g. WANT, INTEND, CHOOSE), or (c) direct perception by the speaker of the state of affairs in the complement (e.g. SEEM, APPEAR, TURN OUT), then it will be subject to transferred negation. This suggestion appears to be consistent with the modal expressions considered here, and with certain others considered below, and may also be a factor in explaining why with MAY NOT the proposition is negated under an epistemic interpretation (i.e. speaker's uncertainty), whereas MAY itself is negated under a deontic interpretation (i.e. speaker's, or other agent's, control). On the other hand, it does not account for why it is that in:

212 It's not possible that p.

it is not the proposition which is negated, unless we regard (212) as an alternative formulation of:

213 It's necessary that not p.

This latter possibility will be referred to again in the following subsection.

5.4.2 *BE POSSIBLE TO/THAT and BE NECESSARY TO(/THAT)*

POSSIBLE represents the objectification of the modal relationship expressed by the modal auxiliaries CAN and MAY, and NECESSARY that expressed by MUST. The distinction between CAN and MAY (cf. 3.3.2) parallels that which exists between POSSIBLE TO (POSSIBLE FOR/TO) and POSSIBLE THAT, and this has been widely recognized, although many have regarded the relationship between CAN and POSSIBLE TO, and that between MAY and POSSIBLE THAT, as one of semantic equivalence; but as we have seen, whereas CAN and MAY are clearly compatible with both subjective and objective readings, the class of expressions to which BE POSSIBLE TO/THAT and BE NECESSARY TO (/THAT) belong can only be objective.

NECESSARY THAT has been referred to only parenthetically, since it rarely occurs in normal usage and is usually restricted to the expression of logical, or alethic, necessity—e.g.:

214 It is necessary that a bachelor be unmarried.

—and it thus belongs to a specialized variety of English. POSSIBLE THAT is also used to refer to alethic possibility, but is not so restricted in its usage. Alethic modality may be regarded as modality that is not relativized to any particular conceptual basis or to any particular set of empirical circumstances—i.e. it is logically idealized and absolute (cf. the discussion of alethic modality in 2.1, and also Kart-tunen (1972) and Miller's (1978: 110) reference to Reichenbach (1947)). However, since this book is concerned principally with the expression of modality in non-specialized English, I will have very little to say about alethic modality.

The adjectives POSSIBLE and NECESSARY can be used attribu-tively (as can many other adjectives which are incorporated in modal expressions—e.g. we can speak of 'sure' winners, 'certain' victory, and 'likely' outcomes) but they nevertheless still appear to qualify second-order or third-order entities. As Hacking (1967: 155) points out, POSSIBLE seems very restricted with regard to the nouns it can modify. 'Possible man', 'possible cat', and 'possible road' are absurd (unlike 'strong man', 'black cat', and 'straight road'), unless we provide some such context as 'a possible man for the job', 'a possible cat for our experiments', or 'a possible road to take to Vanderhoof'. The fact that we are required to do this in order to make sense of POSSIBLE (and the same is true of NECESSARY) indicates that it is not a first-order entity which is being referred to, but a second- or third-order entity—namely, it is possible *that* the man will be suitable for the job; it is possible for us *to* use the cat in our experi-ments; it is possible *to* take that road to get to Vanderhoof. Since this appears to be the case, I will restrict my discussion of POS-SIBLE, NECESSARY, and other modal adjectives to the way they are used within the frame BE . . . TO/THAT.

The core meaning of POSSIBLE TO/THAT may be represented as K(C does not preclude X), where: (i) K = natural/rational laws/C = empirical circumstances/evidence (typically); (ii) C is objective; and that of BE NECESSARY TO as K(C entails X), where (i) K = natural/social laws/C = empirical circumstances/a deontic source; (ii) C is objective.

Much has been made by logicians of the fact that possibility and necessity are interdefinable in conjunction with negative operators. In Aristotle's *De Interpretatione* (Ch. 13, trans. Ackrill, 1963: 62 f.) the following equivalences are expressed:

$$
\begin{array}{rcl}
\text{possible to be} &=& \text{not necessary not to be} \\
\text{not possible to be} &=& \text{necessary not to be} \\
\text{possible not to be} &=& \text{not necessary to be} \\
\text{not possible not to be} &=& \text{necessary to be}^9
\end{array}
$$

and this is reflected in the way that the expressions BE POSSIBLE TO/THAT and BE NECESSARY TO are used in English since there is no transferred negation (cf. 5.4.1).

5.4.3 BE PROBABLE THAT

BE PROBABLE THAT represents the objectification of WILL in most of its non-volitional uses. Its restriction to THAT-complements relates to the fact that it cannot be used deontically. Its core meaning, which can be represented as: K(C is disposed towards X), where (i) K = rational/natural laws/C = evidence/empirical circumstances; (ii) C is objective; (iii) C involves the notion of 'probability', is close to that of BE LIKELY TO/THAT, the latter being perhaps slightly less formal and more biased towards favourability than BE PROBABLE THAT, which is emotively neutral—cf. the difference between a 'likely' winner and a 'probable' winner. This is clearly related to the fact that BE PROBABLE THAT is invariably impersonal—cf.:

215   *He is probable to win.

whereas BE LIKELY TO can occur with subjects in any person.

Also like BE LIKELY TO/THAT, BE PROBABLE THAT is subject to transferred negation—cf.:

It's not probable that he'll win. = It's probable that he won't win.
It's not probable that he won't win. = It's probable that he'll win.

5.4.4 BE APPARENT THAT, BE CLEAR THAT, BE EVIDENT THAT, and BE OBVIOUS THAT

This subcategory of modal expressions is distinguished by the fact that C involves some form of human perception—with an emphasis on visual perception. They therefore express what might be called 'perception' modality, but this is close enough to epistemic modality for the former to be regarded as a particular type of the latter. Each member of this subcategory is, furthermore, restricted to occurring with a THAT-complement. They each share the core meaning K(C entails X), where (i) K = rational laws/C = (perceptual) evidence; (ii) C is objective, and differ as regards whether C involves the observation that X is 'apparent', 'clear', 'evident', or 'obvious'. Each can be negated independently of, and in addition to, the THAT-complement.

5.4.5 BE COMPULSORY TO/THAT, BE IMPERATIVE TO/THAT, BE MANDATORY TO/THAT, BE OBLIGATORY TO/THAT, BE LAWFUL TO, BE LEGAL TO, BE LEGITIMATE TO, and BE PERMISSIBLE TO

Each member of this subcategory is distinguished by the fact that it explicitly expresses deontic modality—which does not necessarily deny the possibility of being used to express dynamic modality by analogy. The first four expressions share the core meaning K(C entails X) and the latter four K(C does not preclude X), where (i) K = social laws/C = a deontic source; (ii) C is objective; (iii) C *explicitly* involves a deontic source; and each expression differs from the others to the extent that the semantics of the lexical items COMPULSORY, OBLIGATORY, etc., may be seen to differ. Whether the expressions in this subcategory can take either a TO- or a THAT- complement, or simply a TO-complement, appears to be related to the semantic consideration of whether obligation (in the case of the first four) or permission (in the case of the latter four) is being expressed.

Permission and obligation appear to be related in the same way as possibility and necessity as shown in 5.4.2 (cf. Leech, 1971: 89 and Lyons, 1977: 832).

5.5 Expressions incorporating verbally-derived adjectives and participles

This category comprises expressions which incorporate past participles which are productively derived from modal lexical verbs, and adjectives which are similarly derived.

5.5.1 Epistemic past participles referring to an act

This subcategory includes the following: BE ADVERTISED THAT, BE AFFIRMED THAT, BE ALLEGED TO/THAT, BE ARGUED THAT, BE ASSERTED THAT, BE ATTESTED THAT, BE AVERRED THAT, BE CLAIMED TO/THAT, BE COMMENTED THAT, BE CONJECTURED THAT, BE DECLARED TO/THAT, BE ESTIMATED TO/THAT, BE HELD THAT, BE HYPO-THESIZED THAT, BE HINTED THAT, BE IMPLIED THAT, BE INFERRED THAT, BE INSINUATED THAT, BE MAINTAINED THAT, BE MENTIONED THAT, BE OBSERVED THAT, BE POINTED OUT THAT, BE POSTULATED THAT, BE PREDICTED THAT, BE PROCLAIMED THAT, BE PROFESSED THAT, BE PROPHESIED THAT, BE PROPOSED THAT, BE RECOUNTED THAT, BE REMARKED THAT, BE REPORTED TO/THAT, BE SAID TO/THAT.

All of the above are used to express epistemic modality and can be used in the frame 'It is . . . that p'. Those followed by TO/THAT can also be used with an infinitival complement in the frame 'NP is . . . to p'. Some of the other expressions which are shown as having only a THAT-complement may also on occasion occur with an infinitival complement, but I have indicated this only when it appears to be a particularly frequent use. Each expression in this subcategory shares the core meaning K(C does not preclude X), where: (i) K = rational laws/C = evidence; (ii) C is objective; and they differ regarding whether C involves reference to an act of advertising, affirming, alleging, etc.

5.5.2 Deontic past participles referring to an act

This subcategory includes the following: BE ADVISED TO, BE ADVOCATED TO, BE ASKED TO, BE AUTHORIZED TO, BE BEGGED TO, BE BIDDEN TO, BE CALLED ON TO, BE COMMANDED TO, BE DEMANDED THAT, BE DIRECTED TO, BE EMPOWERED TO, BE EXHORTED TO, BE FORBIDDEN TO, BE INSISTED THAT, BE INSTRUCTED TO, BE INVITED TO, BE ORDERED TO, BE PERMITTED TO, BE PETITIONED TO, (BE PROHIBITED FROM), BE REQUESTED TO, BE SUPPLICATED TO, BE URGED TO, BE WARNED TO.

Some of the above may occasionally be used with a THAT-complement—e.g.:

216 It's advocated that you leave immediately.
217 It's ordered that you should cease publication.

and BE DEMANDED and BE INSISTED can be used only thus. BE PROHIBITED FROM has been included because of its semantic affinities with the rest, although it can occur only with a gerundive complement.

The core meanings of these expressions are probably best represented in terms of a scale of which the extremes are K(C entails X) and K(C does not preclude X), where: (i) K = social laws/C = a deontic source; (ii) C is objective. Expressions like BE DEMANDED THAT and BE ORDERED TO are clearly near, or at, the former extreme, whereas expressions like BE EMPOWERED TO and BE PERMITTED TO are near the latter extreme. Expressions like BE ASKED TO and BE WARNED TO, on the other hand, appear to be somewhere in between. The core meaning of BE FORBIDDEN TO and BE PROHIBITED FROM may be represented as K(C entails not-X) or as K(C precludes X).

5.5.3 Past participles referring to an epistemic state

This subcategory includes: BE ASSUMED TO/THAT, BE BELIEVED TO/THAT, BE CONSIDERED TO/THAT, BE DOUBTED THAT, BE ENVISAGED THAT, BE FANCIED THAT, BE FELT TO/THAT, BE IMAGINED THAT, BE PRESUPPOSED THAT, BE RECKONED TO/THAT, BE SURMISED THAT, BE SUSPECTED THAT(/OF), BE THOUGHT TO/THAT.

All of these expressions refer to some kind of mental state, as opposed to a particular act, as in 5.5.1, although the distinction is not always clear-cut. In addition to a THAT-complement, BE SUSPECTED may also take a gerundive complement with OF. The core meaning of BE DOUBTED THAT may be represented as K(C does not preclude not-X) and that of the other expressions as K(C does not preclude X), where: (i) K = rational laws/C = evidence; (ii) C is objective; (iii) C = a mental state, and the specific nature of C is explicitly referred to in the past participle. Many of the expressions in this subcategory are subject to transferred negation—e.g.:

$$\text{He's not} \begin{Bmatrix} \text{felt} \\ \text{reckoned} \\ \text{thought} \end{Bmatrix} \text{to be honest.} = \text{He's} \begin{Bmatrix} \text{felt} \\ \text{reckoned} \\ \text{thought} \end{Bmatrix} \text{not to be honest.}$$

5.5.4 Past participles referring to a boulomaic state

Included in this subcategory are expressions such as BE DESIRED THAT, BE FEARED THAT/LEST, and BE HOPED THAT. Each is used to express the specific type of dynamic modality referred to in 2.1 as boulomaic modality. The core meanings of BE DESIRED THAT and BE HOPED THAT can be expressed as K(C is disposed towards X), where: (i) K = psychological laws; (ii) C is objective; (iii) C = the property of human consciousness indicated by the past participle. That of BE FEARED THAT is the same, except that the disposition is negative, as may be explicitly indicated in the archaic complementizer LEST.

5.5.5 Past participles referring to a deontic state

This subcategory includes the following: BE ALLOWED TO, BE COMPELLED TO, BE CONSTRAINED TO, BE ENABLED TO, BE ENTITLED TO, (BE EXEMPT FROM), BE FORCED TO, BE INTENDED TO, BE NEEDED TO, BE OBLIGATED TO, BE OBLIGED TO, (BE PRECLUDED FROM), (BE PREVENTED FROM), BE REQUIRED TO.

Each member of this subcategory refers to the state brought into force by a deontic act, rather than to the act itself, although as noted in 5.5.3, the distinction between such acts and states is not clear-cut in every case. The core meaning of each may be represented as K(C entails X) if some kind of obligation is expressed, and as K(C does not preclude X) if some kind of permission is expressed. In the case of BE EXEMPT FROM, BE PRECLUDED FROM, and BE PREVENTED FROM, however, the core meaning is best represented as K(C precludes X). As was the case with BE PROHIBITED

FROM in 5.5.2, these three expressions are distinguished from the rest of the subcategory on account of the type of complement they take, and this is clearly related to their common meaning of K(C precludes X). In every case (i) K = social laws/C = a deontic source; (ii) C is objective; and (iii) C = the deontic state expressed by the participle.

5.5.6 *BE EXPECTED TO/THAT and BE SUPPOSED TO/THAT*

These two expressions have been included in a subcategory of their own on the grounds that although they closely resemble the expressions in 5.5.3 and their core meaning may be represented as K(C does not preclude X), where K = rational laws/C = evidence, they are also conventionally used in a deontic sense with an effective meaning more like K(C entails X) where K = social laws/C = a deontic source. Their ambiguity can often be used to good effect. For example, in:

218 Every student is expected to pass.
219 Every soldier is supposed to fight to the death.

(218) could be followed either by 'going by their recent form' or by 'or else they can't proceed to the second year'; and (219) could be followed either by 'at least, that's what they say happens' or else by 'in order to defend his country', and in some cases both types of meaning could be intended at the same time, as in:

220 Every man is expected to do his duty.

Both expressions are subject to transferred negation, although when the negative particle occurs immediately before the infinitival complement, the effect is sometimes a little odd—cf.:

She's not expected to come. = She's expected not to come.(?)
You're not supposed to shout. = You're supposed not to shout.(?)

5.5.7 *Epistemic verbally-derived adjectives*

This subcategory includes the following: BE ARGUABLE THAT, BE CONCEIVABLE THAT, BE DEBATABLE THAT, BE DOUBT-FUL THAT, BE PREDICTABLE THAT, BE QUESTIONABLE THAT. Their core meaning may be represented as K(C does not preclude X) where: (i) K = rational laws/C = evidence; (ii) C is objective, but with the exception of BE CONCEIVABLE THAT and BE PREDICTABLE THAT, they all have in addition a strong negative orientation, which is evident in the fact that they can be followed by the complementizer AS TO WHETHER instead of THAT.

5.6 Modal nominal expressions

By 'modal nominal expression' I mean an expression containing a modal noun, and for the purposes of this book I will restrict my comments largely to the occurrence of modal nouns in the frame 'there is a . . . TO/THAT'. Since the expressions in this category are closely related semantically to many of those included in 5.4, I shall discuss them very briefly, and only a few examples of each subcategory will be given.

5.6.1 Epistemic expressions referring to an act

This subcategory includes expressions like: AFFIRMATION, ALLEGATION, ARGUMENT, ASSERTION, CLAIM, COMMENT, CONJECTURE, DECLARATION, HINT, HYPOTHESIS, IMPLICATION, INFERENCE, INSINUATION, OBSERVATION, PREDICTION, PROCLAMATION, PROPHECY, PROPOSAL, PROPOSITION, REMARK, REPORT. Their core meanings may be represented as K(C does not preclude X), where: (i) K = rational laws/C = evidence; (ii) C is objective.

5.6.2 Deontic expressions referring to an act

This includes expressions such as: CALL, COMMAND, DEMAND, DIRECTIVE, EXHORTATION, INSTRUCTION, INVITATION, ORDER, REQUEST, SUGGESTION, SUPPLICATION, WARNING, whose core meanings can be represented along a scale from K(C entails X) to K(C does not preclude X) (cf. 5.5.2) where: (i) K = social laws/C = a deontic source; (ii) C is objective.

5.6.3 Expressions referring to a deontic state

This includes COMPULSION, EXEMPTION, OBLIGATION, and PROHIBITION, whose core meanings can be represented as K(C entails X)/K(C does not preclude X)/K(C precludes X), where: (i) K = social laws/C = a deontic source; (ii) C is objective.

5.6.4 Expressions referring to an epistemic state

This subcategory includes expressions such as ASSUMPTION, BELIEF, CERTAINTY, CONSIDERATION, CONVICTION, DOUBT, EXPECTATION, FEELING, IDEA, NOTION, PRESUPPOSITION, THOUGHT, whose core meanings can be represented as K(C does not preclude X), where: (i) K = rational laws/C = evidence; (ii) C is objective.

5.6.5 Expressions referring to a dynamic (including boulomaic) state

This subcategory includes non-boulomaic expressions like ABILITY, CAPACITY, INCLINATION, LIKELIHOOD, NECESSITY, POSSIBILITY, POTENTIAL, PROBABILITY, whose core meaning can be represented as K(C entails X)/K(C does not preclude X)/K(C is disposed towards X), where: (i) K = natural laws/C = empirical evidence (typically); (ii) C is objective; and boulomaic expressions such as DESIRE, HOPE, WILL, WILLINGNESS, whose core meaning can be represented as K(C is disposed towards X), where: (i) K = psychological laws/C = a property of human consciousness; (ii) C is objective.

Modal nominal expressions represent the ultimate stage in the objectification of modality—namely its nominalization. Modality, as we have seen, is fundamentally a relationship between a set of circumstances and a proposition/event relative to a certain set of laws, but if we are to reflect upon and discuss such a relationship, it must be given some semblance of objectivity, and modal nominal expressions permit more freedom and variety of modification than any other category of modal expressions. Thus while a sentence like:

221 There may be life after death.

allows us to express a modal relationship quite simply, a modal nominal expression permits us to expatiate on such a relationship in infinite detail—cf., for example:

222 The intriguing, unsettling—and even frightening—but evidently irrational possibility of life after death is a cause of anxiety to many.

Note, incidentally, that 'life after death' is essentially a verbal concept, which is obligatory after a modal noun. One could not speak of 'the possibility of a chair'. All modal nominal expressions of the kind being considered here take a verbal complement and the nouns they incorporate thus necessarily belong to only the penultimate rank of 'nouniness' (i.e. that of 'derived nominal') in what Ross (1973) has called the 'Nouniness Squish'.

Notes

1. This is not, in fact, always the case, as is shown by Leech's (1971: 108) example: 'I know him to be an imposter'.
2. I will assume here the univocity of BE in all contexts. Such a view has recently been proposed by Hintikka (1979), who argues that the 'Frege

trichotomy' of the IS of predication, the IS of identity, and the IS of existence is mistaken. He suggests that the tendency of philosophers and linguists since Frege to regard BE as ambiguous is due to their dependence upon first-order logic which differentiates between predication, identity, and existence as 'P(a)', '=' and '∃x'. Hintikka, who employs a semantics which does not depend on first-order logic—namely 'game-theoretical semantics'—shows that BE is univocal in all its uses. However, even if one uses a different semantical system of analysis, he argues, it still remains that 'there does not seem to be a single English sentence which in fact has several readings because of the alleged ambiguity of "is" '.

3. Cf. Bouma's (1975: 325) observation that 'the use of the modal, as opposed to its periphrastic counterpart, allows the speaker to conceal his interpretation of the potential realization of the event. This in effect would mean that the modals are *unmarked* in regard to their periphrastic counterparts'.

4. *Pace* Palmer (1977: 6), who states that 'there is no absolute or logical reason why . . . BE ABLE TO . . . in the past should imply that the event took place'.

5. Cf. Lyons's (1977: 805 ff., 836) discussion and notation for distinguishing between subjective and objective epistemic and deontic modality.

6. Such a combination is by no means peculiar to English. Ultan (1972), for example, reports that the Old Latin future infinitive also consisted of a periphrastic construction denoting goal or purpose, together with the auxiliary 'BE'.

7. Coates (1983: 129) notes that in the corpora she studied, CAN and COULD occurred 14 times more frequently than BE ABLE TO.

8. Negative versions—namely BE UNSURE AS TO WHETHER, BE UNCERTAIN AS TO WHETHER, and BE UNLIKELY TO/THAT—also exist, as do similar versions of many other modal expressions which are negated by means of a prefix, but discussion in this book will be restricted mainly to the non-negative forms.

9. When expressed in this way, the concepts of possibility and necessity appear to be of equal status. However, Lyons (1977: 802, 839) has argued convincingly that 'in English at least, possibility, rather than necessity, should be taken as primitive in the analysis of epistemic modality' but that deontic modality, on the other hand, is necessity based.

6 Modal Adverbs

The category of modal adverbs (which belongs to Greenbaum's (1969: 94 ff.) more general class of 'attitudinal disjuncts') includes the following: ALLEGEDLY, APPARENTLY, ARGUABLY, CERTAINLY, CLEARLY, CONCEIVABLY, EVIDENTLY, HOPEFULLY, MOST/QUITE LIKELY, MAYBE, (NECESSARILY), OBVIOUSLY, PERHAPS, POSSIBLY, PRESUMABLY, PROBABLY, PURPORTEDLY, REPORTEDLY, REPUTEDLY, SEEMINGLY, SUPPOSEDLY, SURELY.

All primarily express epistemic modality (i.e. their core meanings range from K(C entails X) to K(C does not preclude X), where K = rational laws/C = evidence), with the exception of HOPEFULLY (K(C is disposed towards X)), which expresses boulomaic modality (i.e. K = psychological laws/C = a property of human consciousness) and is to be understood here in its more recently acquired sense of 'it is hoped that' (cf. German *HOFFENTLICH*).In fact, most of the modal adverbs are closely related to an equivalent adjectival form (the exception being SEEMINGLY, which is related to IT SEEMS TO/THAT, and MAYBE and PERHAPS) as used in the frames BE . . . THAT and (except in case of APPARENTLY, ARGUABLY, CLEARLY, EVIDENTLY, HOPEFULLY, MAYBE, OBVIOUSLY, PERHAPS, PRESUMABLY, and PROBABLY) BE . . . TO, and they thus retain a strong element of objectivity, like modal adjectives used in attributive position (cf. 5.4.2)—cf.:

He's arguably the most promising newcomer. =
It's arguable that he's the most promising newcomer.
Allegedly, he's the richest man in the world. =
He's alleged to be the richest man in the world.

A few modal adverbs have particular distinguishing features. MOST/QUITE LIKELY clearly differs from the other members of this category as regards its internal structure, but it nevertheless functions quite regularly as a modal adverb.

NECESSARILY has been put in parentheses since, like its adjectival equivalent BE NECESSARY THAT, it is used principally to express alethic modality—e.g.:

223 Bachelors are necessarily unmarried.

which can be glossed as 'it is a logically necessary consequence that
if someone is a bachelor then he is also unmarried', and this use is
not commonly found, except in works on logic. However, the equivalent negative form with NOT is quite common and acceptable—cf.:

224 Bachelors are not necessarily homosexuals.

which may be a consequence of the fact that logically necessary
truths, in so far as they relate to everyday life, are more easily
denied than asserted.[1]

PERHAPS and MAYBE differ from the other modal adverbs in
that they are not unambiguously objective.[2] In fact, like the modal
auxiliaries, they appear to be neutral with regard to the subjective/
objective distinction, which may be largely due to the fact that they
have no adjectival equivalent which can be asserted by means of the
verb BE (cf. 5.1).

SURELY is distinguished from the other modal adverbs in that 'it
is commonly used to invite agreement from the person or persons
addressed' (Quirk *et al.*, 1972: 515). In other words, the addressee
is asked to confirm the speaker's assessment of the truth of the proposition in question.

The semantic characterization of those modal adverbs which have
equivalent adjectival forms is regarded here as being the same as that
of their adjectival equivalent with a THAT-complement and is also
the same as the characterization of their nominal equivalent with a
THAT-complement, if in fact they have one. Thus, for example,
POSSIBLY, IT'S POSSIBLE THAT, and THERE'S A POSSIBILITY
THAT are all regarded here as having the same core meaning. The
differences which do exist between them seem largely due to differences in the way they may be used and in the type of linguistic
unit with which they may co-occur and integrate (cf. Chapter 8).

Modal adverbs differ from modal adjectival expressions and modal
nominal expressions in that they are 'peripheral in clause structure'
(Quirk *et al.*, 1972: 421)—i.e. they are specifically sentence adverbs.
Their peripherality can be seen in the fact that a modal adverb can
appear in a number of different positions within the clause without
affecting the meaning relation between clause and adverb (although
the overall meaning of the resulting sentence may differ). Thus:

225 Possibly, Mr. Smith has been trying to phone us.
226 Mr. Smith has possibly been trying to phone us.
227 Mr. Smith has been trying to phone us, possibly.

and even:

228   Mr. Smith possibly has been trying to phone us.
229   Mr. Smith has been possibly trying to phone us.
230   Mr. Smith has been trying, possibly, to phone us.

can all be paraphrased as:

231   It's possible that Mr. Smith has been trying to phone us.

It may not always be entirely clear that modal adverbs are sentence adverbs. For example, (225) without the comma (i.e. 'possibly' does not have a separate tone group) and with falling intonation on 'Smith' might be interpreted as:

225a   Possibly Mr. Smith, as opposed to Mr. Jones, has been trying to phone us.

and in a sentence like:

232   An evidently irate Mr. Smith is on the line.

EVIDENTLY seems specifically to modify IRATE. However, such 'non-sentential' uses of modal adverbs are more apparent than real, and this can be shown in the same way that modal adjectives were shown in 5.4.2 to be not truly attributive. In order to understand (225) in the sense shown in (225a), it seems clear that we have to construe it as:

(i)   Someone has been trying to phone us.
(ii)   It is possible that this person is Mr. Smith.

and thus POSSIBLY is understood as qualifying a clause, rather than a noun. Similarly, (232) would normally be construed as:

(i)   A Mr. Smith is on the line.
(ii)   It's evident that he's irate.

It has been claimed by Bellert (1977: 343) that 'the modal adverbs have no corresponding negative adverbs that would function as sentential adverbs' and she would thus find an example like:

233   Impossibly, } Mr. Smith has phoned.
       Improbably,

quite unacceptable. However, there is a sense in which (233) is acceptable—namely if it is construed as:

233a   Impossible } though it might seem, Mr. Smith has phoned.
       Improbable

Similarly, a sentence like:

234 An $\left\{\begin{array}{l} \text{impossibly} \\ \text{improbably} \end{array}\right\}$ irate Mr. Smith is on the line.

could be used to convey the information that:

(i)   A Mr. Smith is on the line.

(ii) $\left.\begin{array}{l} \text{Impossible} \\ \text{Improbable} \end{array}\right\}$ though it might seem, he is irate.

It has also been noted by Jackendoff (1972: 84) that modal adverbs 'do not feel comfortable in questions' and stated categorically by Bellert (1977: 344) that they simply 'do not occur in questions'. Thus:

235 Will Mr. Smith $\left\{\begin{array}{l} \text{possibly} \\ \text{probably} \end{array}\right\}$ phone?

would be regarded as 'uncomfortable' by Jackendoff and unacceptable by Bellert. However, (235) could be understood in the sense:

235a Is it $\left\{\begin{array}{l} \text{possible} \\ \text{probable} \end{array}\right\}$ that Mr. Smith will phone?

The question here is used to shift the assessment of truth from the speaker onto the hearer (cf. 9.4).[3]

It is interesting that Bellert (1977: 344) finds the sentence:

236 Have you perhaps misunderstood the question?

quite acceptable and is thus led to infer that PERHAPS is 'not purely modal'. However, although there is clearly a difference in meaning between (236) and a sentence like:

237   Have you possibly misunderstood the question?

this does not mean that we have to regard (236) as 'not purely modal' and (237) as unacceptable. The difference in meaning can be brought out if we paraphrase (236) as:

236a Do you think you have misunderstood the question?

—i.e. non-objective—and (237) as:

237a Is it possible that you have misunderstood the question?

—i.e objective. In other words, it can be seen as a consequence of the inherent objectivity of POSSIBLY and of the neutrality of PERHAPS with regard to objectivity/subjectivity.

On the whole, modal adverbs differ from the modal expressions discussed in Chapter 5 by being far less explicit in the way they qualify the meaning of a clause or sentence. Although some modal adverbs may be premodified—e.g. 'quite possibly', 'very clearly', 'most probably', etc.—the range of potential modifiers is very restricted. Many expressions in Chapter 5, on the other hand, permit a theoretically infinite degree of modification—cf.:

238 It's on the whole somewhat less than likely that . . .
239 It's quite embarrassingly, if not painfully, apparent that . . .

However, what the modal adverbs lack in precision and explicitness is compensated for by their distributional mobility, which enables the modality of a sentence to be not only 'fronted', 'topicalized' or 'thematized', as in (225), but also to be tagged on almost as an afterthought, as in (227), and even to be inserted intrasententially if one should suddenly decide to modalize one's utterance when one is already half way through it, as in (226), (228), (229), and (230).

Notes

1. Cf. Miller and Johnson-Laird (1976: 495): 'logical necessity characterises one domain of discourse, but it is not a domain of preeminent concern to the average person'.
2. Cf. Lyons (1977: 798), who refers to PERHAPS as though it were a subjective epistemic modal expression.
3. Greenbaum (1969: 11) finds the sentence 'Will they possibly leave early?' 'only marginally unacceptable'.

7   Modal Lexical Verbs

Many of the verbs to be included in this category of modal expressions are often discussed under the heading of 'performative verbs'—i.e. verbs which may be used to perform an act, as opposed to merely describing an act or state (cf. Austin, 1962). Here, however, 'performativeness' will be regarded simply as a conventionally determined function of certain verbs when used in the present tense with non-progressive aspect and with a first person subject in a non-negative, non-interrogative environment. In other words, I wish to stress the fact that:

240 I order you to go.

is paradigmatically related to sentences like:

241 I ordered you to go.
242 He orders you to go.
243 Am I ordering you to go?
244 I don't order you to go.
245 You are ordered to go.[1]

The fact that the interpretation of (240) as a command is conventional, rather than being due to any inherent property of the collocation of I and ORDER, can be inferred from the observation that (240) could be uttered to describe an action taking place in a home movie. First and foremost, then, performative verbs *refer to* an act or state which, on certain occasions, may involve the utterance in which the verb is incorporated.[2]

A fairly comprehensive list of performative verbs, which comprise an important subset of what I am here referring to as modal lexical verbs, is given by Fraser (1975: 190 ff.), who includes the following categories:[3]

a. *Acts of asserting*: e.g. AFFIRM, ALLEGE, ARGUE, ASSERT, ATTEST, AVER, CLAIM, COMMENT, CONJECTURE, DECLARE, HOLD, OBSERVE, POSTULATE, PREDICT, STATE, etc.
b. *Acts of evaluating.*[4] e.g. CALCULATE, CONCLUDE, ESTIMATE, GUESS, HYPOTHESIZE, POSTULATE, REGARD, etc.

c. *Acts of stipulating*: e.g. CALL, DECLARE, DESIGNATE, NOMINATE, STIPULATE, etc.
d. *Acts of requesting*: e.g. ASK, BEG, COMMAND, DEMAND, DIRECT, FORBID, INVITE, ORDER, PROHIBIT, REQUIRE, etc.
e. *Acts of suggesting*: e.g. ADVISE, ADVOCATE, EXHORT, SUGGEST, WARN, etc.
f. *Acts of exercising authority*: e.g. ALLOW, AUTHORIZE, EXEMPT, FORBID, PERMIT, PROHIBIT, RULE, etc.
g. *Acts of committing*: e.g. GUARANTEE, PROMISE, SWEAR, UNDERTAKE, VOW, etc.

Many of these verbs will be familiar from Chapter 5, where they were discussed as past participles in the frames BE . . . TO/THAT, and they may also be regarded as modal expressions in their own right as full verbs, since they indicate that the truth of a proposition/ occurrence of an event is relative to some circumstance which, in the case of the verbs looked at so far, involves a specific act, either previous or current (although it can be a state, as we shall see below) in accordance with a set of socially defined laws. The meaning of such verbs can thus be represented in terms of the core semantic frames K(C entails X), K(C does not preclude X), and K(C is disposed towards X), where K = social/rational laws and C = a deontic source/evidence.

Such a view clearly conflicts with that of Ross (1970) and others who have argued that *all* sentences are derived from an underlying structure containing a performative verb. Thus for Ross the following two sentences:

246 I assert that all men are mortal.
247 All men are mortal.

are synonymous and differ simply in that in (247) 'I assert' has been deleted. In the present account, on the other hand, it is being proposed that (246) is a modalized version of (247) and that the two are therefore clearly different in meaning. That this is so can be shown by the fact that (246) and (247) have different entailments. Fodor (1977: 57) points out that whereas:

248 All men are mortal.
    Socrates is a man.
    _____

    Socrates is mortal.

is a valid argument, the equivalent with (246)—namely:

249 I assert that all men are mortal.
  I assert that Socrates is a man.
  _____
  I assert that Socrates is mortal.

is a nonargument.[5] The reason why this is so is that while (247) asserts that 'All men are mortal', (246) asserts that 'X asserts that all men are mortal'. (247) asserts the truth of a proposition, whereas (246) asserts the assertion of the truth of a proposition.

There is a sense, of course, in which a categorical assertion like (247) is relative to the speaker's utterance of it (cf. Lyons, 1982), but the important point is that this relativity is not formally explicit. As Fodor (1977: 57) would put it, a sentence like (247) 'conveys' the assertion that 'All men are mortal' without actually 'expressing' it. Similarly,

250 Go forth and multiply.

might be uttered, and interpreted, as a command, although it is not *explicitly* a command since it could also be used as an exhortation, request, etc. Performative verbs are used in cases where it is important to specify the exact status of an utterance within a given social or rational system. In uttering a categorical assertion or directive, a speaker does not explicitly align himself with any moral, institutional or other set of rules or values. Such utterances will almost invariably be uttered in some social context, but the fact that they are formally categorical will usually mean that any social rules are contextual. An utterance such as:

251 I claim that Smith is a murderer.

is significant in that it makes the truth of 'Smith is a murderer' relative to a system K of social/rational laws in which it is important to differentiate between acts of claiming, on the one hand, and acts of affirming, swearing, suggesting, prophesying, hypothesizing, etc., on the other. In (251) the use of the verb CLAIM identifies the specific circumstance to which the truth of the proposition is relative as an act of claiming, and the co-occurrence of CLAIM with I helps to identify the fact that it is the utterance of (251) itself which is to be thus identified.

There are a considerable number of modal lexical verbs which do not necessarily have to occur before their complement. These have been termed 'parenthetical verbs' by Urmson (1952: 481), who defines them as verbs 'which, in the first person present, can be used . . . followed by "that" and an indicative clause, or else can be inserted at the middle or end of the indicative sentence'. Lyons (1977: 738) feels that 'it would seem to be desirable to widen the definition of parenthetical verbs offered by Urmson so that it includes performative verbs used parenthetically'. There are, however, a large number of performative verbs which occur with an infinitival or a gerundive complement, rather than with a THAT-complement, and some of these are often rather odd, if not entirely unacceptable, in parenthetical position—cf.:

252 I order you to hand over the money.
253 Hand over, I order you, the money. (?)
254 Hand over the money, I order you. (?)
255 I exempt you from having to pay.
256 From having, I exempt you, to pay. (?)
257 From having to pay, I exempt you. (?)
258 I authorize you to leave early.
259 You may, I authorize, leave early. (?)
260 You may leave early, I authorize. (?)

If one wished to widen Urmson's definition of parenthetical verbs and still exclude examples like the above, it would probably be necessary to exclude all verbs which can co-occur only with infinitival and gerundive complements. Leaving Urmson's definition as it is still enables us to include a large number of performative verbs—namely those which can occur with a THAT-complement—cf.:

261 You are, I declare, quite mad.
262 You are quite mad, I declare.
263 He did not, I claim, have any right to insult her.
264 He did not have any right to insult her, I claim.

although even some of these can appear a little strange—e.g.:

265 You are living, I assert, beyond your means. (?)
266 You are living beyond your means, I assert. (?)

Those verbs which are most at home with Urmson's definition are those such as the following, which appear to refer more to a mental state or attitude than to a specific act and are not, therefore, used performatively: ASSUME, BELIEVE, FANCY, FEAR, FEEL, GUESS, HOPE, IMAGINE, PRESUME, RECKON, SUPPOSE, SURMISE, SUSPECT, TAKE IT, THINK, TRUST, UNDERSTAND.[6]

These verbs are all used to express either epistemic or boulomaic modality (i.e. K = rational/psychological laws and C = evidence/a property of human consciousness) and thus both in meaning and in syntactic versatility they have a close affinity with the class of modal adverbs (Chapter 6), which can be seen in the following:

267 He's drunk again, I presume.
268 He's drunk again, presumably.
269 Evidently she's not coming.
270 I take it she's not coming.
271 He's reputedly a millionaire.
272 He is, I understand, a millionaire.

Parenthetical verbs would typically be used with a first person subject in the present simple tense, although this does not have to be the case—cf.:

273 This was, she felt, a little too much to bear.
274 This was to be the end, they thought.

The impersonal constructions IT APPEARS and IT SEEMS clearly also belong in Urmson's class of parenthetical verbs.

Some parenthetical verbs are subject to transferred negation in initial position—cf.:

275 I don't believe he's coming.
276 I don't imagine they'll ever get married.
277 I don't think you're up to it.

That it is, in fact, the complement clause that is negated in such cases can be ascertained by attaching a tag to the sentence. As Akmajian and Heny (1975: 21) have pointed out, the appropriate tag for:

278 I don't expect John will sing the songs.

is not 'do I', but 'will he'.

It is also significant that when such verbs occur in medial and final position they can be negated only if the complement clause is also negated—cf.:

279 *He's coming, I don't believe/expect/imagine/suppose/think.
280 He's not coming, I don't believe/expect/imagine/suppose/think.

Interestingly, in the latter case, despite the fact that the parenthetical verb does not appear to be negated, the two negatives acting upon the complement clause do not cancel out.

Another class of modal lexical verbs which are not used performatively are those which refer to a boulomaic state—e.g. WANT NP TO, YEARN FOR NP TO, LONG FOR NP TO, or to a non-boulomaic state—e.g. REQUIRE, NEED. The following:

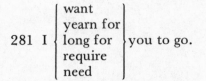

281 I { want / yearn for / long for / require / need } you to go.

all relate the putative occurrence of the addressee's going to a current state, rather than to a previous or current act.

Notes

1. This type of expression has, of course, already been discussed in Chapter 5.
2. A similar view is taken by Fawcett (1980: 127), who argues that 'all performative verbs, . . . whether or not used "performatively" (i.e. in the first person singular with present simple tense in a non-embedded clause) should be handled in the grammar in exactly the same way as any other lexical verb'.
3. I have not included Fraser's 'Acts of reflecting speaker attitude'—e.g. APPLAUD, CONGRATULATE, CONDEMN—which, on the whole, are represented by factive predicates and are therefore concerned with a state of the current actual world, rather than a possible state of the world (cf. 2.1).
4. Note that the sense of 'evaluate' here is not the same as that of 'evaluative' in Rescher's category of evaluative modality discussed in 2.1—i.e. Fraser's sense does not imply factivity.
5. For a version of this and other counterarguments to the performative hypothesis, see Levinson (1980).
6. Lyons's claim, as stated above, seems to be based on the misunderstanding that this is the only type of verb that Urmson intended to be captured by his definition. In fact, the 'definition' quoted by Lyons—namely, verbs used in the first person of the simple present tense 'to modify or weaken the claim to truth that would be implied by a simple assertion'—was not intended to be a full definition of the term 'parenthetical verb'. As Urmson (1952: 481) clearly states: 'the features of parenthetical verbs to which I shall draw attention are only one aspect of their use'.

8   Synopsis of Modal Expressions

The survey of English modal expressions in Chapters 3 to 7 is intended to be exploratory rather than exhaustive. Many sub-categories are represented by only a few examples, and there are a considerable number of internally complex adverbial expressions— e.g. IN SOME CIRCUMSTANCES, IN MY OPINION, AS I AM GIVEN TO UNDERSTAND, SPEAKING AS A HOUSEWIFE AND MOTHER OF THREE—which are clearly modal in nature but which have not been discussed at all. It has not, however, been my intention to provide a complete grammar of English modal expressions, but rather to establish a basic semantic framework for such a grammar which makes it possible to assess whether an expression can be regarded as modal or not, and if it can, what kind of modality it expresses and precisely how it expresses it. I have attempted to show, therefore, what all modal expressions have in common, while at the same time suggesting a number of ways in which individual modal expressions may differ. The account of modal expressions presented so far has thus been largely expository. What I will do in this chapter is use the above exposition as the basis for a possible explanation of why it is that such a wide range of modal expressions is available in English, and why it is that the modal auxiliaries are so often singled out as somehow being more 'central' to the expression of modality in English than other modal expressions.

First of all, consider the use of the modal auxiliary MAY in the following sentence:

282   He may go.

(282) is ambiguous with regard to a 'possibility' or 'permission' interpretation—i.e. which interpretation is intended is not formally explicit.[1] (282) is furthermore vague[2] since under the 'possibility' interpretation it could refer, for example, either to the present or to the future, and the modality expressed could be either sub-jectively or objectively epistemic; and under the 'permission' inter-pretation the source of the permission could be either the speaker or not the speaker. (282) would typically be uttered, therefore, under circumstances where the context of utterance was such as to

disambiguate it and where its vagueness was either similarly contextually resolved or else was unimportant.

If the context of utterance is insufficient to resolve such ambiguity and vagueness and the speaker does not wish to leave them unresolved, there are a number of options open to him. Let us assume, first of all, that he wishes to make an explicitly objective epistemic modal assertion. He can do so by using IT'S POSSIBLE THAT, or POSSIBLY, or THERE'S A POSSIBILITY THAT, or IT'S CONCEIVABLE THAT, etc., and here he must make a further choice regarding whether he wishes to use a present simple tense—namely:

283
$\left.\begin{array}{l}\text{Possibly} \\ \text{It's possible that} \\ \text{There's a possibility that}\end{array}\right\}$ he goes.

or a non-actual (future) tense—namely:

284
$\left.\begin{array}{l}\text{Possibly} \\ \text{It's possible that} \\ \text{There's a possibility that}\end{array}\right\}$ he will go.

POSSIBLY, IT'S POSSIBLE THAT, and THERE'S A POSSIBILITY THAT are, as we have seen, inherently objective. If the speaker wishes to specify a tense but to leave the subjective/objective distinction inexplicit, he may say instead something like:

285 Perhaps $\left\{\begin{array}{l}\text{he goes.} \\ \text{he will go.}\end{array}\right.$

If, however, he wishes to make the modality of his utterance explicitly subjective, he may use a modal lexical verb with a first person subject, although he is obliged here to specify further the nature of the subjective epistemic state. He may, for example, choose one of the following:

286 I $\left\{\begin{array}{l}\text{think} \\ \text{believe} \\ \text{reckon}\end{array}\right\}$ $\left\{\begin{array}{l}\text{he goes.} \\ \text{he will go.}\end{array}\right.$

A slightly less varied range of choices faces the speaker if, instead of epistemic modality, he decides to express deontic possibility—i.e. permission. If he wishes to make an objective deontic statement or directive he may use expressions like:

287 It is $\left\{\begin{array}{l}\text{permitted} \\ \text{permissible}\end{array}\right\}$ for him to go.

288 Permission is/has been granted for him to go.

Here, there is no need to specify a tense, since the complement clause is infinitival. If the speaker wishes to indicate that he is the deontic source, he may say something like:

289 I $\left\{\begin{array}{l} \text{permit} \\ \text{allow} \\ \text{authorize} \end{array}\right\}$ him to go.

If one chooses an adjectival or nominal expression to convey either epistemic or deontic possibility, one has the further option of being able to modify it with an adverb if it is adjectival—e.g.:

290 It is quite possible that he will go.
291 It is unfortunately permitted for him to go.

and with an adjective if it is nominal—e.g.:

292 There's a remote possibility that he will go.
293 There's a presidential authorization for him to go.

If one chooses to express epistemic modality by means of a modal adverb, one has the choice of either 'thematizing' the modality, as in:

294 Possibly he will go.

'interpolating' the modality, as in:

295 He will possibly go.

or 'adjoining' the modality, as in:

296 He will go, possibly.

When the modality is expressed by means of an adjectival or nominal expression it is, of course, always thematized.

The set of options given above is summarized in Figure 8.1. This represents only a few of the choices open to a speaker who wishes to express epistemic or deontic possibility—a similar set of choices is also available if he wishes to express dynamic possibility. Modal adverbs and lexical verbs may also be modified, though less freely than modal adjectival and nominal expressions, and most options allow for a far wider range of realizations than those shown in Figure 8.1. What is most significant about Figure 8.1 is that it affords clear confirmation of Bouma's (1975: 325) suggestion, as noted in 5.1, that 'the modals are *unmarked* in regard to their periphrastic counterparts'. The modal auxiliaries are, in fact, the least formally explicit of all modal expressions. That is to say that they convey no more information than that there exists a certain relationship

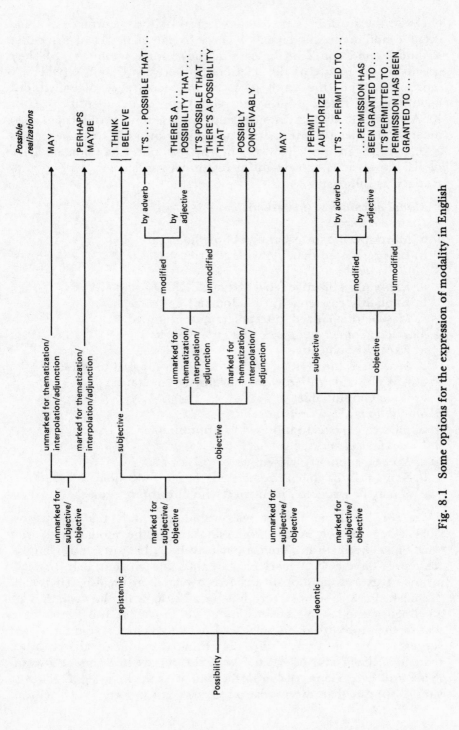

Fig. 8.1 Some options for the expression of modality in English

between the truth of some proposition p or the occurrence of some event e and some circumstance C relative to some set of principles K (and a condition Z in the case of the secondary modals). All they specify is the nature of the relationship between C and X (where X represents either the truth of p or the occurrence of e) without including any direct information about the actual identity of C or X. All the non-auxiliary modal expressions, on the other hand, do incorporate specific information about one or more of the variables X, C, and K. The principal ways in which auxiliary and non-auxiliary modal expressions tend to differ in formal explicitness may be summarized as follows:

1 *Modal auxiliaries*: unmarked
2 *Quasi-auxiliaries*:
   a. More specific information about the nature of C
   b. Less restricted than (1) with regard to tense
3 *Modal adverbs*:
   a. Explicitly objective (apart from PERHAPS and MAYBE)
   b. Explicitly epistemic (or boulomaic)
   c. May be thematized, interpolated, or adjoined
4 *Modal adjectival and participial expressions*:
   a. Explicitly objective
   b. More versatile than (1), (2), and (3) with regard to tense
   c. C is often identified with a specific act or state
   d. Widely modifiable
5 *Modal nominal expressions*:
   Similar to (4) except more widely modifiable
6 *Modal lexical verbs*:
   a. May be explicitly subjective
   b. Some may be thematized, interpolated, and adjoined
   c. C may be explicitly identified with current utterance

We can see from this broad outline why it is that of all possible categories of modal expressions, it is the modal auxiliaries which have been studied almost exclusively by linguists: quite simply, they provide the least marked, and thus the most straightforward, means of expressing modality that is available in English. Their lack of markedness is almost certainly bound up with the fact that of all English modal expressions they are the most fully integrated within the structure of the clause. Lyons (personal communication) suggests that 'the more fully something is grammaticalized rather than lexicalized and integrated with the syntax in terms of government and agreement, the more central it is in the system'. Thus it would appear that the modal auxiliaries are indeed more 'central' in English than non-auxiliary modal expressions, which tend to be realized lexically, and are thus grammatically more peripheral.

The notion of syntactic centrality and the scale of formal explicitness of modal expressions also recalls Ross's (1972) notion of 'category squish' according to which verbs, adjectives, and nouns form a continuum along which verbs represent an extreme of syntactic volatility, nouns an extreme of syntactic inertness, and adjectives are somewhere in between. The account proposed here suggests that a number of the syntactic phenomena in terms of which such a category squish is described may well be semantically and pragmatically motivated.

Notes

1. For a definition of formal explicitness, see 2.4.
2. I am following Kempson's (1977: 123 ff.) distinction between vagueness and ambiguity, which is that a verb phrase may be regarded as ambiguous if, when it is conjoined to a DO SO or other verb phrase pro-form expression, the overall meaning of the sentence is also ambiguous, whereas it is merely vague if the main verb and the pro-verb can each bear a different interpretation.

9 Further Ways of Expressing Modality in English

9.1 Introductory

Up to now I have been concerned almost exclusively with expressions as a means of realizing modality. There are in addition, however, a number of linguistic devices in English which can be used to express modality which are not, strictly speaking, expressions in the sense defined in 2.4. In order to give some semblance of completeness to the view of modality which is being elaborated in this book, I will look briefly in this chapter at a number of such devices and relate them to what has been proposed so far.

9.2 Tense

It was noted in 2.1 that time can be regarded as a modality in its own right in so far as a non-current state of the actual world may be understood in terms of its existence in a world which differs from the current actual world. Rescher (1968: 25), as we have seen, includes temporal modalities such as 'It is sometimes the case that p', 'It is always the case that p', and 'It was yesterday the case that p' in his list of modalities. The linguistic device most frequently associated with the expression of time reference in English is tense, although we have seen that with the secondary modal auxiliaries at least, time reference is only one of several subfunctions of the so-called 'past' tense.[1] It has also been noted in 3.3.3 that although WILL is probably best regarded as a modal expression which may incidentally refer to future time, it has nevertheless often been analysed as a future tense morpheme in the same way that -ed is often analysed as a past tense morpheme. Long (1961: 188), for example, observes that 'from the point of view of syntax, the use of auxiliaries is not really different from the use of other inflectional devices. Thus the separate *will* of *George will probably start tomorrow* is syntactically quite like the attached *ed* of *I started yesterday*'.

Whether one regards time as a modality or not, it is certainly significant that those linguistic devices which are most frequently regarded as referring to past and future time in English are also used to express modalities which are not specifically temporal. Because of the traditional association of tense with time reference, the use of tense to refer to time, as in:

297 If I *said* that, you would hit me.
298 I wish you *lived* nearer.
299 Pretend there *was* a ladder on top and y- and then they *lowered* the ladder like that—mm and then they *climbed* up *lowered*— and *highered* the ladder and *sat* on the ladder. (Fawcett and Perkins, 1980.)
300 I *thought* I'd come with you, if you don't mind.

has often been felt to be atypical in some way. In all four examples given above, the 'past' tense form has little, if anything, to do with past time, since in each case it refers to a non-past state of affairs. The reason we know this is that it is specifically indicated contextually. In (297) the 'past' tense morpheme correlates with an unreal condition signalled by IF. An unreal condition is similarly signalled by WISH in (298)—and in fact a 'past' tense appears to be obligatory in complements following WISH (except when it is used in the specific sense of 'making a wish')—cf.:

301 *I wish you live nearer.
302 *I wish you will live nearer.

Examples like (299) are common in the speech of children, as has been pointed out by Lodge (1979) and Kaper (1980). The 'pretend world' is clearly non-actual and unreal, as opposed to past and real, and in (299) and other such examples, the tense of the verbs, either in conjunction with PRETEND or merely in an appropriate context, is sufficient to indicate this.

That (300) does not refer to past time (at least directly) can be clearly seen by comparing it with its 'present' tense equivalent —e.g.:

303 I think I'll come with you, if you don't mind.

The difference between (300) and (303) is one of politeness rather than of time reference, and the 'past' tense of THOUGHT in (300) reflects the tentativeness, or even embarrassment, of the speaker.

There appears, then, to be little, if any, difference between the function of the tense morpheme in (297)–(300) and its function in the secondary modal auxiliaries (cf. 3.4)—i.e. it represents a conditional feature Z to which the truth/actuality of a proposition/ event is relativized in accordance with a set of laws K. But can this analysis be extended to *all* the uses of tense?

The view that tense is essentially a device for expressing modality has recently been proposed independently by Lyons (1977) and Kress (1977). Lyons (1977: 819 f.) suggests that 'what is customarily treated as being primarily an opposition of tense—past vs. non-past —in English and other languages, should be more properly regarded as a particular case of the distinction, remote vs. non-remote ("then" vs. "now" being a particular case of "there" vs. "here"). Under this interpretation, tense would be a specific kind of modality; and modality would be more closely related to deixis'. Kress (1977: 48 f.) similarly argues that the so-called present tense is used to denote actuality, certainty, and validity, whereas the -ed morpheme denotes unreality or non-actuality, social distance or non-validity.

One consequence of such a view is that the specific type of remoteness which a given -ed morpheme is intended to convey cannot be determined independently of context. Thus a sentence like:

304 He went home.

clearly expresses remoteness, but what kind of remoteness will vary from context to context—cf.:

305 He went home last night.
306 Let's pretend he went home.
307 I hope he went home.
308 If he went home, he would be better off.
309 I'm worried in case he went home.
310 What if he went home yesterday?
311 What if he went home tomorrow?

The upshot of this is that a past time reference interpretation will be due to the occurrence of an -ed morpheme in a factive context—as represented by 'last night' in (305)—and a non-actual or counterfactual interpretation will be due to the occurrence of an -ed morpheme in a non-factive context—as represented by PRETEND, HOPE, IF, IN CASE, and WHAT IF in (306)–(311). Similarly, a present-time reference interpretation of a sentence will be due to a combination of non-remoteness and factivity, and a future time reference interpretation will be due to a combination of non-remoteness and non-factivity.[2] It would thus appear that the analysis of so-called past tense proposed in 3.4 for the secondary modals can be extended such that *all* uses of the -ed morpheme may be characterized as a condition Z whose identity must be contextually specified.

The notion of non-factivity incorporated in modal expressions is often specifically identified with the modal auxiliary WILL. Anderson

(1971:96), for example, suggests that epistemic '*may* (and *can*) and *must* are derived from alternative underlying structures, one containing a "predictive" category (in the underlying subordinate clause) written out in the "full versions" as *will*, the other lacking this category'. This has been formalized in some versions of transformational grammar (e.g. Rosenbaum, 1967) as a rule of WILL-deletion. Thus a sentence with a non-factive infinitival complement such as:

312   I expect to go.

would be regarded as being derived from an underlying structure like:

312a I expect—I will go.

WILL is an obvious choice to represent non-factivity, since it is one of the least formally explicit modal expressions, and in certain contexts may be interpreted as little more than an index of non-factivity—cf.:

313   He'll be the man who's come to tune the piano.

WILL still remains, however, one among many expressions which can be used to indicate non-factivity, and it has been shown (e.g. by Jenkins, 1972) that WILL-deletion is far too simplistic to account for the many and varied ways of expressing non-factivity in English. Jenkins (1972: 175) argues, for example, that WILL-deletion would be expected to apply in a case like:

314   I know that the Red Sox will do well tomorrow.

to give:

314a   *I know that the Red Sox do well tomorrow.

whereas it obviously can't. With a verb like HOPE, on the other hand, there appear to be no such restrictions—cf.:

315   I hope that the Red Sox will play the Yankees tomorrow.
315a I hope that the Red Sox play the Yankees tomorrow.

Instead of a rule of WILL-deletion, Jenkins argues instead for a rule of WILL-interpretation.

  In the present account, the unacceptability of (314a) can be explained on the grounds that KNOW is a factive verb (cf. the discussion of epistemic modality in 2.1) and one is not rationally able to know a future event. (314) is acceptable, however, since one can know that circumstances are disposed towards the occurrence of a future event—the inclusion of WILL indicates that factivity is not being claimed for the complement. In (315) and (315a) no such restriction occurs, since HOPE is a modal (i.e. non-factive) verb.

It was suggested in 3.4 that an *-ed* morpheme (or a 'remoteness' morpheme, as it might be called) could be regarded as a device used to 'increase' the modality of a modal expression in that it indicates that X (which is already relative to C within the system K) is further relative to a condition Z. Thus, just as:

316 Do it next Tuesday.

is less modal than:

317 You can do it next Tuesday.

due to the presence of the modal expression CAN, so (317) is less modal than:

318 You could do it next Tuesday.

due to the presence of the *-ed* morpheme in (318). The modality of (318) can be further increased by including the auxiliary HAVE -EN, as in:

319 You could have done it next Tuesday.

In (319) HAVE -EN has little to do with temporal reference— it is used simply as a further index of modal remoteness. The increase in modality from (316) to (319) can correlate directly with an increase in tentativeness/politeness/formality, depending on the context of utterance.

9.3 IF-clauses

The particle IF is another linguistic device which enables the speaker to qualify his commitment to the truth of a proposition or the actuality of an event. Quirk *et al.* (1972: 747) liken IF-clauses to questions in that they 'imply uncertainty about the actual existence of the circumstances referred to'. In fact, IF (like WHETHER) can be used in conjunction with a verb like ASK to report a question, as in:

320 He asked me if I needed anything.

IF-clauses are usually discussed in terms of their function as the protases of conditional sentences, in which they may be used to signal an 'open' (Quirk *et al.*, 1972: 747) or 'real' (Leech, 1971: 110) condition, as in:

321 If you don't like it, that's your hard luck.

322 If he was hard on you, it was in your own interests.

or else a 'hypothetical' (Quirk *et al.*, 1972: 747) or 'unreal' (Leech, 1971: 110) condition, as in:

323 If you were really hungry, you wouldn't refuse stale bread.
324 If I'd seen him do it, I would have called the police.

In the case of (321) and (322) there is no indication as to whether the condition is (or will be) fulfilled or not, whereas in (323) and (324) it is implied that the condition is not fulfilled. Conditional sentences, however, can also be expressed without the help of an IF-clause, as can be seen in:

325 Should you not like it, that's your hard luck.
326 Had I seen him do it, I would have called the police.

where inversion of subject and auxiliary verb performs the same function. The view of IF preferred here, then, is that like subject-auxiliary inversion, and like the *-ed* morpheme it is more accurately regarded as an index of 'conditionality' in the much broader sense suggested in 3.4—i.e. as an index of modality—since this enables us to account not only for the use of IF in conditional sentences like (321)-(324), but also for its use in sentences like the following:

327 See if I care!
328 What if they've been killed?
329 I don't know if he's coming yet.
330 You look as if you've been dragged through a hedge.

IF may therefore be regarded as a modal particle.

9.4 Questions

Questions may also be regarded as a means of conveying modality in so far as they may be defined semantically as the expression of a speaker's ignorance or doubt (C) with regard to the truth of a proposition or the actuality of a state of affairs (X) relative to rational laws (K). For example, in order for a yes–no question to be uttered felicitously, it must be the case that 'the speaker doesn't believe that the proposition is true, but does believe that it may be true . . . , and believes that the addressee is at least as likely as he is to know whether it is true' (Hudson, 1975: 7). Since questions qualify the truth of a proposition by making it relative to the speaker's uncertainty, they may be regarded as expressing epistemic modality, and in particular 'addressee-oriented' epistemic modality.[3]

Such an analysis, however, holds only at the level of semantics. Pragmatically and ontogenetically (cf. 11.2) the basic function of questions appears to be to elicit some kind of response from an addressee. Fawcett (1980) uses the term 'information seeker' instead of 'question', but from the broadest perspective, questions may be regarded as a means of seeking more than just information. Goody (1978b: 26) suggests that 'the direct illocutionary force of all questions is the elicitation of a response—but not necessarily a verbal response' and in her analysis of interrogative modes in Gonja she isolates not only 'information-seeking questions', but also 'rhetorical questions', i.e. 'questions for whose answers the information channel is effectively empty'; 'control questions', i.e. questions used to control the behaviour of others; and 'deference questions' which 'by at least *seeming* to ask for information, [imply] ignorance by the questioner of the answer'.

Nevertheless, the notion of qualification or guardedness inherent in a broad interpretation of the concept of modality is still apparent in such functional categories when contrasted with the use of straightforward statements or commands for similar ends. It would be a mistake, however, to regard the formal realizations commonly associated with questions—namely WH-words, subject-auxiliary inversion, DO-support, and rising intonation—as exclusively modal linguistic devices, as is apparent in the following:

331 What an ugly wound!

(i.e. the use of WH-words in 'exclamatives'—cf. Hudson, 1975: 8)

332 She likes algebra, and so do I.

(i.e. inversion after SO, and DO as a pro-verb)

333 They say he eats worms, which he does.

(i.e. DO used as a pro-verb in an elliptical 'confirmative tag' (cf. Darden, 1973))

334 Little does he know what lies in store.

(i.e. DO as a lexically empty particle after the 'minimizer' LITTLE (cf. Quirk *et al.*, 1972: 453)).

Similarly, rising intonation, which is often associated with questions, is by no means to be uniquely identified with the meaning of 'polarity unknown' as Halliday (1970c: 23, 26) seems to suggest. For example, if one's name is called, one may well respond by saying 'Yes' or 'Mm' with a rising intonation. To interpret this as 'I am uncertain as to the polarity of what you have said or are about to say' would be to read far too much into it. A more satisfactory pragmatic interpretation might be that the rising tone simply represents an invitation from the speaker to the addressee to deliver his message, although the whole issue of the range of modal attitudes which intonation may be used to express is extremely complex (cf., for example, Crystal, 1969 and 1975).

There is a particular subclass of questions known as 'deliberative' questions in which the speaker puts himself in the role of both speaker and addressee, and thus the truth of the proposition is seen as relative to the worldview of the speaker in his addressee role. The 'deliberativeness' of deliberative questions does not have to be made formally explicit, and thus:

335 Can pigs fly?

could be deliberative if the condition that the speaker was addressing himself were met. As Lyons (1977: 756) points out, a deliberative question is 'first and foremost a mental act', but such questions may be verbalized and their 'deliberativeness' made explicit by means of the modal lexical verb WONDER, as in:

336 Can pigs fly, I wonder?
337 I wonder whether pigs can fly.
338 Could you speak a little louder, I wonder?
339 I wonder whether you could speak a little louder.

WONDER invariably expresses epistemic modality, but in a case like (338) or (339) it would be usual for the utterance to have the overall illocutionary force of a request, and I WONDER would be used in such a case to express an extra degree of politeness.

Yes–no questions may also be used to qualify or 'tone down' a direct command, as in:

340 Go away, will you!
341 Stop that racket, can't you![4,5]

One possible explanation of such sentences is that the main imperative clause is effectively transformed into the topicalized complement of a yes–no question, and thus the focus is shifted away from the speaker as deontic source and on to the addressee as the source of information relevant to the truth of the proposition in question. Such an interpretation of sentences like (340) and (341) would account for Hudson's (1975: 28 f.) observation that the restrictions which make the following unacceptable:

342 *Don't let's have any more, won't you?

343 * Let's have some more, shan't we?
344 * Let's not have any more, shan't we?

also apply to 'full interrogatives' used 'imperatively':

345 * Won't you not have any more?
346 Shan't we have some more? (?)
347 * Shan't we not have any more?

If this analysis is correct, then 'will you' in (340) and 'can't you' in (341) are not to be regarded as proper tag questions at all.

There seems to be no reason, however, why we should not regard the following as tag questions:

348 Shirley's your sister, isn't she?
349 Shirley's your sister, isn't she?
350 Shirley isn't your sister, is she?
351 Shirley isn't your sister, is she?
352 Shirley's your sister, is she?

(cf. Quirk *et al.*, 1972: 390 ff.) Hudson (1975) has argued that tag questions do not need to be analysed any differently from full interrogatives, and they do indeed appear to be equivalent in expressing addressee-oriented modality. However, the fact that they appear in parenthetical position, like modal adverbs and parenthetical modal lexical verbs, can often make the addressee orientation of tag questions appear a little tentative.[6] A further parallel between tag questions and modal adverbs and parenthetical verbs is that the former, like the latter two, may sometimes occur in medial position with similar effect. Just as a modal adverb may be inserted intra-sententially 'if one should suddenly decide to modalize one's utterance when one is already half way through it' (Chapter 6) so Corum (1975: 139) notes that a tag question may sometimes occur in the middle of a sentence where 'the speaker has started off a statement that immediately sounds too strong, so he sticks in the tag to soften it' and gives as an example:

353 That was a stupid thing, wasn't it, for Custer to do.

One may conclude, then, that although it may not be the primary function of questions to express modality, the various affinities between questions and other linguistic devices whose primary function appears to be to express modality suggests that questions are far more central to the discussion of modality than is often thought to be the case.

Notes

1. Cf. Kruisinga (1932: 527): '[ED] , as far as it is used as a predicative form, is as much a mood as a tense'. Cf. also the view of Young (1980) that 'tense makes the proposition compatible with reference to certain periods of time', rather than referring to time itself.
2. This characterization of time reference in terms of remoteness and factivity is due to Lyons (1977: 820).
3. Cf. the distinction referred to in Turner and Pickvance (1972: 93) between 'ego-centric' expressions of uncertainty such as I THINK, and 'socio-centric' expressions of uncertainty such as ISN'T IT.
4. Cf. Leech's (1977: 142) pragmatic definition of 'fracturing': 'a command retrospectively softened by a request'.
5. CAN and WILL and their secondary equivalents COULD and WOULD are the only modals which can be used in such cases, which is related to the fact that they are effectively the only modals which can be 'subject oriented' (cf. 3.3).
6. Lakoff (1972b: 917), for example, claims that 'a tag question is really intermediate between a statement and a question: a statement assumes that the addressee will agree, and a question leaves the response of the addressee up to him, but a tag question implies that, while the speaker expects a certain sort of response, the hearer may not provide it'.

10 Modal Expressions and Politeness

In this book the concept of modality provides a unifying basis for bringing together within a single perspective a wide range of expressions and other linguistic devices which in many cases have previously been regarded as being quite unrelated. That so many different linguistic phenomena may be encompassed within a single semantic framework may be an interesting fact in itself and, arguably, this might be regarded as sufficient justification for the analysis proposed above. In this chapter, however, I will attempt to show in addition that many of the various distinctions established on semantic and syntactic grounds are also motivated pragmatically.

In 3.4 several pragmatic scales were proposed as being relevant to the interpretation of the semantic feature which distinguishes the secondary modal auxiliaries from their primary counterparts. It was suggested that the degree of modality formally explicit in a modal expression is directly proportionate to the distance of the expression from the leftmost extreme of one of the following scales:

non-hypothetical———————————hypothetical
non-past———————————past
non-formal———————————formal
non-polite———————————polite
non-tentative———————————tentative
non-indirect———————————indirect

The particular scale with which an expression correlates depends, of course, on the context of utterance. We have now established a wide range of various linguistic devices which may be used to express modality, and if the analysis is at all accurate, it should in principle be possible to state for any given modalized sentence not necessarily what scale it correlates with but, given that it does correlate with one or more of the above scales, where it is to be located relative to another modalized sentence. Thus if:

354 He may be mad.
355 He may possibly be mad.

are both uttered in similar contexts with the intention of expressing tentativeness, (355) should be more tentative than (354), since it contains an additional modal expression. By the same token, if a sentence like:

356 It's possible that he is mad.

is uttered in a context similar to that of (354) and (355) and is compared with (354) in terms of formality, one would expect (356) to be more formal than (354), since (356) explicitly conveys objective epistemic modality, whereas in (354) the subjective/objective distinction is left vague. In this latter comparison, however, it is the type of modality which differs, rather than the degree of modality, and although this appears to have some reflex in the pragmatic dimension of formality, (354) and (356) appear to be virtually equivalent in terms of the non-hypothetical–hypothetical scale.

To the extent that modality can be seen to correlate with such pragmatic scales, the syntactico-semantic analysis of the various means of expressing modality in English proposed in Chapters 3 to 9 should provide us with a formal basis for analysing a number of pragmatic phenomena. In this chapter I propose to concentrate on one pragmatic phenomenon in particular—namely, politeness— and will attempt to show how the analysis of modality given above illuminates both the concept of politeness and the way it functions in human interaction.

The expression of politeness is usually referred to only incidentally in linguistics. It is often noted that a specific form is more polite than, or a polite equivalent of, another; but systematic studies of the expression of politeness are rare, the major contribution to date being that of Brown and Levinson (1978), who examine in considerable detail the concept of politeness itself and the various types of linguistic expression used to convey politeness in a wide variety of languages. Modal expressions, however, are not singled out for any special treatment, but of the five general categories of politeness strategy proposed by Brown and Levinson (e.g. p. 65) it seems clear that modal expressions are used in the service of one strategy in particular—namely, 'negative politeness', which is defined as 'redressive action addressed to the addressee's negative face: his want to have his freedom of action unhindered and his attention unimpeded' (Brown and Levinson, 1978: 134). One other linguistic treatment of politeness is that of Lakoff (1972b), who shows that modal auxiliaries and tags, which are formally unrelated, may both be used to convey politeness; but these are virtually the only two types of expression she considers. The fact that both of these are, according to the present account, types of modal linguistic device is a preliminary confirmation of the connection between modality and politeness. However, modal auxiliaries and tags are, as we have seen, by no means the only devices used to express modality in English, and in this chapter I will try to show how the entire range of modal devices available in English may be used to express politeness and, further-more, that a number of the syntactico-semantic distinctions established above between different categories of modal expressions are reflected in the way they are used to convey politeness.

As noted above, it has often been recognized that the modal auxiliaries may be used to soften the force of an assertion or a directive. Fraser (1975: 196), for example, notes that MUST 'can be used to relieve the speaker agent of some of the responsibility for the consequences of whatever he is obliged to do: it is a way of getting off the hook. Thus when the speaker utters a sentence like ['I must conclude that you are not interested'], he is predicating the obligation to perform the particular act and, at the same time, implying that he would like to be relieved of at least some of the onus of the consequences'. MAY would probably be generally con-sidered more polite than MUST both in its epistemic and deontic sense, on the grounds that possibility and permission are less com-mittal than necessity and obligation. Compare, for example:

357 She may have schizoid tendencies.
358 She must have schizoid tendencies.
359 You may stop writing now.
360 You must stop writing now.

(358) makes a far stronger claim than (357), and (359) allows the addressee a wider range of options[1] than (360).[2] I have already noted as well (in 3.3.2) that a request of the form:

361 May I speak to the manager?

would generally be regarded as more polite than:

362 Can I speak to the manager?

probably as a result of the persistent tendency to regard CAN as primarily a dynamic modal.

Since the secondary modal auxiliaries are 'more modal' than their primary counterparts (cf. 3.4) on account of the further condition indicated by their tense form, it follows that they are also potentially more polite. This prediction appears to be borne out by the follow-ing examples where the 'b' form is more polite than the 'a' form, given identical contexts:

363a Will you let me have a look?
363b Would you let me have a look?
364a Shall we think about going home now?
364b Should we think about going home now?
365a You must cut down on your drinking.
365b You ought to cut down on your drinking.
366a May I just have one little peep?
366b Might I have just one little peep?
367a Can you tell me the way to the station?
367b Could you tell me the way to the station?

Such predictions of the relative politeness of a modal expression can never, of course, be absolute, since they depend to such a large extent on the particular context of utterance. Lakoff (1972b: 910 ff.) argues, in fact, that:

368 You must have some of this cake.

is more polite than:

369 You should have some of this cake.

and also:

370 You may have some of this cake.

when spoken at a party by a hostess offering the guests a cake she has baked or selected herself, whereas one would normally predict that (368) would be *less* polite than (369) and (370). Lakoff's explanation is that the use of MUST in such a context would be interpreted as meaning that 'the thing the addressee is told to do is distasteful to him: he must be compelled to do it against his will', whereas with SHOULD and MAY 'there is normally no assumption that the action is to be performed against the subject's will'. Palmer (1979a: 170), on the other hand, suggests a far simpler and more plausible explanation—namely that 'it is the duty of a hostess to persuade her guests to take as much food as possible', and thus the more persuasive she can be, the more she is carrying out her duty towards her guests. Hence in this case even the use of a straight imperative such as:

371 Have some more cake.

would be entirely acceptable.

However, despite the existence of such contextual constraints on judgements of relative politeness, it is still possible to predict the relative politeness of modal expressions on semantic grounds.

Whether or not the primary semantic basis of expressions of politeness is contextually overridden in certain cases is, as Palmer (1979a: 170) puts it, 'more a matter for sociology than linguistics'.[3]

It was suggested above that one major difference between the modal auxiliaries and most other modal expressions is that the former are neither inherently subjective nor objective, whereas the latter are predominantly inherently objective, and this difference also plays a part in the expression of politeness. Compare the following, for example:

372 You must wear evening dress to the reception.
373 You have to wear evening dress to the reception.

The use of HAVE TO in (373) implies that the deontic source is not the speaker, whereas MUST in (372) leaves the identity of the deontic source open. This distinction can be exploited as a difference in the degree of politeness expressed in the following way. By implying that he is not the cause of the obligation (whether, in fact, he is or not) as in (373), the speaker manages to inform the addressee that such an obligation exists, without taking any personal responsibility for it. In (372), the speaker does not deny that he is personally responsible, and when contrasted with (373), (372) may be regarded as virtually an admission that the speaker is responsible. (372) is thus far more intrusive and direct than (373) and imposes more upon the addressee.

If the speaker wished to make it clear that he was directly responsible for the obligation, there are a number of ways he might go about it. Firstly he could use the modals WILL or SHALL as in:

374 You will wear evening dress to the reception!
375 You shall wear evening dress to the reception!

As noted in 3.3.3, the use of WILL and SHALL to express deontic modality (i.e. K = social laws/C = a deontic source) ensures that the deontic source is the speaker and no one else, and that the utterance containing WILL or SHALL is itself the deontic act. Consequently, (374) and (375) would normally be interpreted as being less polite than either (372) or (373). A further way of admitting responsibility would be to use a modal lexical verb in the first person singular, as in:

376 I require you to wear evening dress to the reception.

and in principle (376) would also be less polite than (372) and (373), since the more explicitly subjective a modalized directive is, the more it imposes the personality of the speaker upon the addressee, and thus the more it is likely to deny the equality of speaker and addressee and provoke interpersonal friction.

The same phenomenon is apparent in the difference in function between active and passive sentences—thus:

377 You are ordered to leave.

would generally be regarded as more polite (formal) than:

378 I order you to leave.

The relationship between a scale of subjectivity–objectivity and one of impoliteness–politeness which is being proposed is not merely speculative, since there is some experimental evidence which suggests that objectivity and politeness go hand in hand. Fielding and Fraser (1978) report that a sample of Bristol University undergraduates tended to use more nominal expressions when addressing an unfamiliar listener and more verbal expressions when speaking to a familiar listener. If their results are accurate, one should in theory be able to predict a scale of politeness such as:

less polite   You shall go.
⬆   You must go.
│   You have to go.
⬇   You are obliged to go.
more polite You have an obligation to go.

As Brown and Levinson (1978: 212) note, it seems that 'in English, degrees of negative politeness (or at least formality) run hand in hand with degrees of nouniness'. (Cf. the comments in Chapter 8 on 'centrality' and 'nouniness'.)

The fact that modal expressions may combine with one another means that any sentence may in theory be made more or less polite by the addition or omission of a modal expression (provided that it is used as a means of not imposing on the addressee), and this means that it is possible to make a rough assessment of the relative politeness potential of a given sentence by counting the number of modal expressions it contains. Cf., for example, the apparent increase in politeness in the following:

less polite   Stop writing.
⬆   It's necessary for you to stop writing.
│   It may be necessary for you to stop writing.
│   It may possibly be necessary for you to stop writing.
│   I imagine it may possibly be necessary for you to stop
│   writing.
⬇   I would imagine it may possibly be necessary for you
more polite to stop writing.

Note that the more modal expressions that are included, the more difficult it is to construe the sentence as a directive, and the number of modal expressions is therefore also an index of the indirectness of a directive. This correlates with politeness in that the inclusion of modal expressions will in theory make it easier for the addressee not to regard the utterance as a directive, if he should feel so inclined —the decision as to how the utterance is to be interpreted is left up to him. If he does interpret the utterance as a directive but does not wish to obey it, he has grounds for not doing so, since he may argue that the utterance is not a directive at all.

This suggests a pragmatic explanation for why:

379 Can you please shut the door?

is acceptable, but:

380 *Are you please able to shut the door?

is not.[4] Leech (1977: 142) describes PLEASE as a 'marker of politeness when the speaker wants a favour from the addressee', and it follows that such a device will be used only when the speaker intends to make it quite clear that he *is* asking a favour. Thus:

381 Please shut the door.

is acceptable since the utterance will clearly be a directive. (379) is also acceptable since, although it is less obviously a directive (without PLEASE) than (381), it is still conventionally interpretable as a directive. (380), on the other hand, is not readily interpretable as a directive—it is more objective than (379) and would be used, as opposed to (379), in a situation where the speaker wanted to make it easier for the addressee *not* to regard it as a request for a favour. The inclusion of PLEASE in (380), therefore, conflicts with the speaker's intention not to make it as obvious as in (379) and (381) that his utterance is a directive as opposed to a request for information. It also follows that a sentence like:

382 *Can it be possible that you are please able to shut the door?

will be even more unacceptable than (380), since it is even less obviously a directive.

(379), (380), and (382) are all what Holmberg (1979) calls A-indirectives (cf. the discussion in 2.2), as opposed to a sentence like:

383 It's cold in here.

which is a B-indirective, if uttered with the intention of getting someone to shut the door. Since B-indirectives are in principle more difficult to construe as directives than A-indirectives, it would follow that (383) is potentially more polite than (379). (379) is explicitly a categorical assertion, but if it were modalized, one would naturally expect it to be even more polite if still used with the same directive function, since it would not simply be an explicit assertion, but a tentative assertion in addition. One may therefore predict the following scale of politeness:

less polite	Shut the door.
↑	Can you shut the door?
	It's cold in here.
	It appears to be cold in here.
↓	One might say that it were cold in here.
more polite	One might have said that it appeared to be cold in here.

So far I have been mainly concerned with the use of modal *expressions* to convey politeness, but much the same can be said of tense, IF-clauses, and questions which, as we saw in Chapter 9, may also be regarded as ways of expressing modality.

It is the feature indicated by the tense morpheme incorporated in the secondary modal auxiliaries which makes them potentially more polite than their primary counterparts, and it was further- more shown in 9.2 that the only apparent difference in meaning between the following:

384 I think I'll come with you, if you don't mind.
385 I thought I'd come with you, if you don't mind.

is that (385) is more polite than (384).[5] Naturally, in a context where the 'remoteness' morpheme correlates with past time reference, as in:

386 I met a lot of friends in the pub yesterday.

it has nothing to do with politeness which, it should be remembered, is only one pragmatic correlate of tense, and thus (386) is no more or less polite than:

387 I meet a lot of friends in the pub every day.

We have also seen in 9.3 that IF may be regarded as a modal particle, and there are some occasions on which the only reasonable interpretation of the meaning of IF is that it is being used to convey politeness. For example:

388 If I could just make one final point . . .

389 If you could call round here, then, and we'll go in my car.

are essentially 'rhetorical' requests for permission and are roughly equivalent, respectively, to:

390 Could I just make one final point?
391 Could you call round here, then, and we'll go in my car?

Presumably, there is some ultimately recoverable apodosis in (388) and (389) such as 'I would be happy', but it seems more reasonable to regard the use of IF in such cases simply as a polite concession towards the addressee, who is not expected to refuse the speaker's request.

   IF-clauses are often used parenthetically after an explicit apodosis as a means of giving options to one's addressee—cf.:

392 I'll have another piece of cake, if you don't mind.
393 I'll be going now, if that's all right.

and PLEASE, one of the most common politeness signals in English, is itself ultimately derived from an IF-clause—namely, 'if you please' (cf. French 'S'il vous plaît').

   Questions (cf. 9.4) are eminently suited for allowing an addressee his freedom of action, however they are expressed. Thus:

394 Will you give me a cigarette?
395 Give me a cigarette?

are both more polite under similar circumstances than:

396 You will give me a cigarette.
397 Give me a cigarette.

   The considerable difference in politeness between interrogative and non-interrogative indirect requests using modal auxiliaries has been experimentally verified by Mohan (1974), whose results include the following:

398 You can open the window. (3.40)
399 Can you open the window? (2.50)
400 You will open the window. (4.80)
401 Will you open the window? (2.07)

The figures in parentheses represent a politeness rating according to a test carried out by Mohan on eighty subjects in the age range 18–35 with equal numbers of males and females. The plain imperative:

402 Open the window.

was ranked as 3.00, and any score higher than 3.00 is relatively less polite, and any score lower than 3.00 is relatively more polite. In (400) (whether we interpret it as K = rational laws/C = evidence, or as K = social laws/C = a deontic source) the addressee is given little option of refusal. (398), on the other hand, leaves the addressee's options more open. There is a correspondingly greater swing towards politeness between (400) and (401) than between (398) and (399), since in the former case, a far greater degree of autonomy is given to the addressee as a result of the role reversal.

For the moment we may conclude that modality and politeness are extremely closely related—so much so that there appears to be a direct relationship between, on the one hand, the degree of formal explicitness of a given modal expression and the type of modality it expresses and, on the other, the degree of politeness it conveys. I will come back to the general significance of such a relationship in Chapter 12.

Notes

1. Cf. Brown and Levinson's definition of negative politeness above.
2. It might be argued that a scale of tentativeness would be more suitable than one of politeness in comparing (357) and (358), but under the broad definition of politeness being used here, tentativeness may also be a manifestation of politeness. It is true, nevertheless, that the use of modal expressions in directives, such as (359) and (360), is more easily interpretable as politeness, given a minimum of contextual information, and most of the examples given below will be of this type.
3. See Gibbs (1981) for a more detailed account of the role of context and convention in the interpretation of indirect requests.
4. A number of different explanations have been proposed to account for this. For example, Gordon and Lakoff (1971) would argue that the occurrence of PLEASE in (379) but not in (380) is a syntactic constraint controlled by the conversational postulate which interprets (379) as a request. Sadock (1974), on the other hand, argues that a request/imperative performative occurs in the semantic structure of (379), but not in that of (380). Neither of these would appear to be entirely satisfactory. For several counterarguments, see Leech (1977).
5. Sheintuch and Wise (1976: 555 f.) give syntactic reasons for regarding I THINK as simply a politeness device in some contexts. They point out that 'I think she eats nothing for breakfast' would normally be unacceptable, since NEG-attraction (nothing = not something) applies only with expressions which denote sureness on the part of the speaker. However, if the sentence were spoken by a nurse reminding a doctor that a patient is not supposed to have any breakfast—i.e. she is not expressing uncertainty about what she is saying, but merely being polite because of the doctor's status—then it would be acceptable.

11   Modal Expressions in Child Language

11.1 Introductory

Much of the discussion in previous chapters has been devoted to arguing that modality is a single semantic system consisting of a relationship between a small number of variables, and that this single system underlies a wide variety of formally heterogeneous expressions and other linguistic devices. I have also tried to demonstrate, however, that there are good reasons why such a wide range of variations on a basic theme should exist—for example, certain forms may be used when the nature of the C variable is evident from the context of utterance (e.g. the modal auxiliaries), whereas other forms (e.g. modal adjectival and participial expressions) incorporate specific information about the identity of the variable; some expressions (e.g. HAVE TO) require only a very broad understanding of social constraints, whereas others (e.g. modal lexical verbs) presuppose a reasonably sophisticated knowledge of social rule systems and role relationships; some forms presuppose no more than a relatively undifferentiated awareness of the empirical world (e.g. CAN), whereas others are far more precise in this respect (e.g. BE ABLE TO, HAVE THE CAPACITY FOR); some forms do little more than signal non-factivity (e.g. TO), whereas others require an awareness of the fact that non-factivity is contingent rather than absolute (e.g. IF); and yet others incorporate the reasons for non-factivity (e.g. IT IS PROPOSED THAT, I THINK); finally, while some expressions (e.g. epistemic MUST) involve the laws of reason only implicitly, others (e.g. I INFER THAT, IT IS HYPOTHESIZED THAT) require a fairly explicit knowledge of human reasoning processes.

Since modal forms vary with regard to the degree and sophistication of knowledge of the natural, rational, and social laws which they presuppose, it is at least possible that there may be some correlation between the cognitive capacity of an individual and the linguistic means at his disposal for expressing modality, and one might also predict that a young child, whose knowledge of such areas is necessarily highly restricted, would differ radically from an adult in his expression of modality. Thus although the adult system would have much in common with the child system, the latter would presumably not include modal devices of more than a given degree of 'complexity', where 'complexity' may be measured in terms of the degree of specification of the C variable and the degree of knowledge required about natural, social, and rational laws. In addition, given the immensity of the task of acquiring a tolerably adequate understanding of such laws, one would predict that the mastery of a fully developed modal system would not be achieved until relatively late in a child's developmental schedule, and that this would be reflected in his use of modal expressions.

The questions raised by considering the development of modality in the broad sense which is being proposed here cover an uncomfortably large area of developmental psychology: the acquisition of modal devices cannot be dissociated from the child's social, moral, and general intellectual development, and any satisfactory treatment of these issues is clearly beyond the scope of this chapter, although I will at various points make tentative suggestions as to how certain aspects of child development may illuminate, or be illuminated by, the present approach to the analysis of modal devices in English. My main aims (which are somewhat narrower) in this chapter will be to trace the way in which the expression of modality in English changes as children grow older and, following the pattern established above, to try to relate the acquisition of a number of formally distinct linguistic devices which are semantically similar in that they may be used to express modality.

There has not been a great deal written on the development of the expression of modality as such, and in order to build up some kind of unified picture it will be necessary to draw upon a variety of sources where modality is often treated only incidentally, and there will inevitably be a number of more specific areas about which very little can be said at all. A further problem is that most of the literature on child language development has been concentrated on the pre-school years, and in particular the period up to the age of about 3. In order to redress the balance a little, I have carried out a fairly detailed study of various modal expressions in a large corpus of spontaneous conversation among 6- to 12-year-old children, which I recorded as part of the Polytechnic of Wales Language Development Project.

In 11.2 and 11.3 I will trace the developmental course of modal expressions first in the language of pre-school children (i.e. up to the age of approximately 5 years) and then in the language of primary school children (up till the age of 12 years). In 11.4 I will propose an analysis of this developmental process, partially based on the framework proposed in Chapters 3 to 9.

11.2 Modal expressions up to the age of 5

The appearance of modal auxiliaries—the first English modal expressions to be acquired—in children's spontaneous speech is well documented. Round about the age of 2;0 CAN and sometimes WILL appear, but only in their negative forms CAN'T and WON'T (cf., for example, Leopold (1949), Ervin (1964), Klima and Bellugi (1966: 194), Brown *et al.* (1969), Bloom (1970), and Slobin (1971), but it is commonly accepted that at this early stage CAN'T and WON'T (and also DON'T) are simply used as unanalysed negative morphemes, on a par with NO, and are not to be regarded as a combination of a modal auxiliary verb with a negative particle, since they clearly have no such significance for the child, who has no positive forms to contrast them with (cf. Kuczaj and Maratsos (1975: 108 f.), Fletcher (1979: 267), and Smith and Wilson (1979: 214)).

Within a month or two of the appearance of CAN'T and WON'T, however, the child begins to show evidence of an awareness of the distinct lexical items CAN and WILL, although individual children may differ in the routes they take to such awareness. W. R. Miller (1973) reports that in the speech of one child, Susan, at age 2.2, almost all yes-no questions contained one of the modals COULD,[1] WILL, and CAN, which apparently functioned as politeness devices. By 2.5, however, there was evidence that WILL and CAN were being used productively, since they appeared in both inverted and non-inverted sentences and in negative environments. Four other children that Miller (1973) studied manifested the apparently more typical strategy of using CAN and WILL in negative environments *before* using them in yes–no questions. Kuczaj and Maratsos (1975) report another strategy used by Abe, who used modals productively in affirmative sentences before he used them in yes–no or WH-questions. But whatever route a child may take, there seems to be considerable agreement among researchers that the modals used most frequently, and in many cases exclusively, by children at this stage are CAN and WILL[2] (and sometimes SHALL in first person interrogatives). Fletcher (1979: 280 f.), for example, reports that the only modal forms found in the spontaneous speech of Daniel between 2;0 and 2;2 were CAN, CAN'T, WILL, WILLN'T, and SHALL. These were used in affirmative, negative, and interrogative environments, as exemplified in the following:

Affirmative:	I can come in your bed.
(You go and tell mummy:)	I will.
Negative:	I can't open my bag.

(Eat your toast:)	I willn't.
Interrogative:	Can I blow the candles out, can I?
	Shall I do that?

The evidence reported so far is based on what was observed in the spontaneous speech of young children, but there is also evidence that children know a good deal about modal auxiliary verbs even before they use them. Kuczaj and Maratsos (1975) found that Abe was able to imitate declarative (but not interrogative) modal auxiliary sentences and to differentiate between grammatical and ungrammatical examples at a stage when the only spontaneous evidence of knowledge of the modals was his use of monomorphemic CAN'T. Later, Abe began to use CAN and WILL in declarative sentences, but none of his interrogative sentences contained them; but in a further set of imitation tests carried out between 2;9;16 and 2;9;19 he correctly imitated grammatical yes–no questions and normalized ungrammatical ones, and also correctly imitated ungrammatical WH-questions and normalized grammatical ones in a way consistent with the incorrect spontaneous WH-questions he was yet to produce—e.g.:

403 What can a skinny snake wiggle really fast?

was imitated as:

404 What a skinny snake can wiggle really fast?

Kuczaj and Maratsos suggest that their results count as evidence for some kind of preanalysis on the part of the child: although he has considerable knowledge of a certain item or structure, he will not use it productively until he feels he has mastered it.

It is important to note that although WILL and CAN are usually being used productively by about 2;6, they are used in a far more restricted way than in the adult system. Fletcher (1979: 282) notes that 'the modals used at this stage are without exception interpersonal and action-oriented'. His data shows that Daniel 'is either using the modal for himself (to indicate willingness, inability, or request for permission), or to allow or prohibit an action by his addressee. He does not use modals to refer to the willingness or ability of third persons'. Wells (1979), who studied the development of the English auxiliary system in a sample of 60 children between the ages of 15 and 42 months, reports that 50 per cent of the sample had used WILL at least once in an 'intend' sense by 2;6, in a 'predict' sense by 3;0, and in a 'performative request' sense by 3;0; and had used CAN at least once in an 'ability' sense by 2;6, and in a 'performative permission' sense by 2;9. However, CAN had not attained the 50 per cent criterion in its 'performative request' or 'constraint' senses by 3;6. It is often extremely difficult to give a precise interpretation of the sense in which a given modal is being used, even with older children (cf. 11.3.4), and it is all too easy to credit a child with a greater degree of sophistication than he in fact possesses—and Wells' data conflicts, for example, with that of Shields (1974: 189), who found that WILL in its 'predictive' sense was used only sporadically up to the age of 3;6—but as Wells includes no examples, one must reserve judgement on this matter. What *is* clear from Wells' data, however, is that the modals in the language of young children are restricted in their usage and that the same form is used to express a wider range of meanings as the child grows older.

The acquisition of modal forms other than CAN and WILL is far less well documented, the two major sources being Shields (1974), who provides the data shown in Table 11.1 which is based on a study of 5,232 verb phrases in the speech of 107 children between the ages of 2;6 and 4;11; and Wells (1979), whose findings are shown in Table 11.2. Bearing in mind that Wells' data only covers the period up to 3;6, the two tables represent a reasonably consistent picture, the only outstanding difference being the extremely high incidence of HAVE GOT TO in Wells' data and its infrequency in Shields' data over the same period.

According to Shields' data, WILL/SHALL and BE GOING TO are used with equal frequency in the speech of children from 2;6 to 2;11, although by the second half of the fourth year WILL/ SHALL is being used more than twice as frequently as BE GOING TO. However, it is not clear how far young children differentiate between the two forms. Kuczaj and Maratsos (1975: 93) note that Abe was using GONNA and WANNA in contexts like:

405 I gonna go.
406 I wanna go.

at a time when other non-negative modal expressions were virtually non-existent in his speech.

MUST, MAY, and the secondary modals WOULD, COULD, MIGHT, SHOULD, and OUGHT TO are used far less frequently than CAN, WILL, SHALL, and BE GOING TO (and HAVE(GOT)TO, according to Wells) although the odd exception can occur.[2] This is clearly in need of some explanation (and one will be proposed in 11.4), since tense is marked productively on main verbs before the secondary modals are used (cf. Fletcher, 1979: 273). Kuczaj and

Table 11.1 Percentage of total verb forms with modal and quasi modal
auxiliary constructions

		2;6–2;11	3;6–3;11	4;6–4;11
1	Will, shall, won't	2.4	4.8	6.5
2	Can, can't	3.2	5.4	4.9
3	Must, should	—	0.9	0.8
4	Would, could	—	0.7	2.0
5	Going to	2.4	2.7	3.1
6	Have to, got to	—	0.7	1.6
7	Had better	0.8	0.3	0.4

Source: Shields, 1974: 186.

Table 11.2 Distribution of auxiliary forms

	Total frequency	Proportion of sample using	Age in months at criterion
Can	1,210	98	30
Will	841	100	30
Be going to	512	92	33
Have got to	232	73	36
Shall	123	60	39
Could	66	50	42
Have to	55	42	
Must	52	45	
Might	32	32	
Should	26	25	
Would	25	22	
May	25	17	
Had better	23	25	
Would like to	20	17	
Be able to	3	5	
Ought	2	3	

Source: Wells, 1979: 257.

Daly (1979: 572) report that the use of WOULD is shaky even
after the age of 5. Although many children will use WOULD in
short replies to an adult's question containing WOULD, they tend
to revert to WILL in longer replies, as in the following example from
a child age 3;7, cited by Kuczaj and Daly (1979: 273):

407 *Adult*: Who would have to feed the horse?
     Child: I would get some hay. I will get some water and hay
        and he will drink the water and he will eat the hay.

Shields (1974: 195) also notes that in the earlier part of her sample, WOULD is usually supplied only in answer to hypothetical questions. When she administered a test to forty children from the sample between the ages of 3 and 5, in which each child was asked to repeat twenty affirmative sentences containing modal forms (and it should be noted that not every child completed the test), 'in the records of children under three there were phonological confusions of *will/would, can/could* and *shall/should* in several cases and at least four clear substitutions. *Must* was substituted by *have to* in four cases and *ought to* by *have to* in one . . . The substitutions show a grasp of underlying meaning, but there appeared to be some evidence that the more hypothetical forms *would* and *could* were still tied to *will* and *can* to the extent that the pronunciation was not properly differentiated'.

Hirst and Weil (1982) found that children between 3;0 and 6;6 understood the modals MUST, MAY, and SHOULD in their epistemic sense before their deontic sense. This is a somewhat surprising finding in that both Kuczaj (1977) (cited by Hirst and Weil) and Wells (1979: 258) found that these modals were *used* first in a deontic sense.

Age is not the only factor relevant to the acquisition of secondary modal forms. Turner and Pickvance (1972: 105) report that out of thirty middle-class 5-year-olds who were asked a question with MIGHT, 43 per cent took over MIGHT into their answer, whereas not one of eight working-class children, to whom similar questions were addressed, used MIGHT in their reply. Turner and Pickvance also appear to be the only researchers who have looked at children's usage of modal expressions other than modal auxiliary verbs, although they only studied 5-year-olds and were principally interested in the effect of social class on linguistic output. They distinguish between 'ego-centric sequences' such as I THINK, and 'socio-centric sequences' such as YOU KNOW, YOU SEE, ISN'T IT?, etc. (cf. Bernstein, 1962), and also examine the use of questions, 'refusals'—i.e. I DON'T KNOW, I CAN'T THINK—modal auxiliaries and adjuncts, and expressions like LOOK AS IF/AS THOUGH/LIKE, which they call 'suppositions based on perception'. Their findings enable us to build up a general picture of what one might call the 'modal competence' of 5-year-olds, although one must bear in mind that the data was obtained in conversation with an adult and was not always spontaneous. Their results may be briefly summarized as follows:

1 I THINK tended to be used more by middle-class than working-class children.

2 Of the socio-centric sequences, the YOU KNOW/SEE type were extremely rare, whereas reversed polarity tags were common but used by significantly more middle-class than working-class children.

3 There was no class difference in the use of direct questions, although more children of the medium verbal ability group than of the high verbal ability group asked them. With indirect questions (e.g. I WONDER . . .), on the other hand, social class was again the major differentiating factor, since they were asked more by middle-class than working-class children.

4 More middle-class than working-class children gave refusals.

5 Modal adverbs and modal lexical verbs other than I THINK (e.g. SUPPOSE, GUESS) were virtually non-existent.

6 Modal auxiliaries were common, but out of 80 subjects, 9 middle-class children used modals like COULD and MIGHT in ascriptive clauses concerned with particular concrete entities—e.g.:

408 Might be a tunnel.
409 Could be a funny aeroplane.

whereas no working-class children did.

7 Use of suppositions based on perception were more frequent in middle-class children's speech than in working-class children's speech.

It is clear from Turner and Pickvance's findings that children from middle-class backgrounds will tend to be slightly ahead of children of the same age from working-class backgrounds in their use of modal expressions.

So far I have looked only at the development of modal *expressions* in the language of children under 5, but there has also been a limited amount of research carried out on the development of tense, IF-clauses, and questions which, as was seen in Chapter 9, may also be regarded as a means of expressing modality.

In 9.2 tense was regarded as essentially a modal device, and there is some support for this view in the child language literature. The first 'past' tense forms to appear are irregular ones like CAME, WENT, DID, etc. (Brown, 1973: 358 f.), but since no -ed forms occur at the same time with regular verbs, it seems reasonable to regard them as tenseless single morphemes. Regular past tense forms usually appear towards the end of the second year (i.e. about 1;9), but there is strong evidence that they are not used in the same way as -ed forms in the adult language. Antinucci and Miller (1976: 182), for example, interpret data obtained from Italian and English children as showing that 'the child is able to make reference to and encode past events only when their character is such that they result in a present end-state of some object' since, at first, children appear to mark only for past verbs such as FALL, OPEN, WIPE, etc., which indicate a change of state. Thus at this stage, it is argued, the past 'tense' has more of an aspectual than a temporal value. This aspectual use of tense has also been noted in the language of French-speaking children by Ferreiro and Sinclair (1971: 46). Such a difference between child and adult use of tense is hardly surprising when one considers that pre-school children appear to be unable to 'decenter' (cf. 11.4) temporally until about 4;6 (Cromer, 1971), and the use of appropriate adverbials to specify past tense forms (as noted by Crystal, 1966) in young children's speech is rare and inconsistent (cf. Fletcher, 1979: 271). Antinucci and Miller (1976: 187), therefore, find it more illuminating to regard children's first use of 'past' forms, such as the Italian imperfect and English *-ed*, as expressions of 'non-actuality' rather than 'pastness'. Italian children, for example, at first use the imperfect almost exclusively for story-telling where the stories are predominantly imaginary, as opposed to narrations of past events. Antinucci and Miller regard the use of the past tense to refer to past time as a later specialized development of the more general meaning of non-actuality, although as Lodge (1979) and Kaper (1980) note, the expression of non-actuality remains an important function of the 'past' tense.

With reference to Antinucci and Miller's hypothesis, Fletcher (1979: 272) strikes a note of caution, suggesting that 'an argument of this kind based entirely on spontaneous speech data and the analyst's semantic classification runs a risk of circularity', but it is nevertheless interesting that the view of tense proposed in 3.4 and 9.2—namely that the English *-ed* morpheme essentially denotes deictic remoteness which may, depending on context, be interpreted in terms of temporality or non-factivity—seems well suited to describing the development of tense and time reference in child language.

The view of IF proposed in 9.3 also appears to provide a suitable framework for accounting for the development of IF-clauses, in that its suggested modal meaning appears to be ontogenetically basic. IF is comparatively rare in spontaneous speech before the age of 5 (cf. Emerson (1980: 139) who also cites evidence from Menyuk (1969) and Kuczaj and Daly (1979)), and Emerson (1980: 151) found that the children she tested 'did not appear to differentiate logical and illogical sentences with *if* prior to 6;11–8;7'. However, before the child comes to associate unidirectional event order with IF, he apparently understands it in the sense of 'contingency', although he is still generally unable to appreciate that the event referred to in an IF-clause is necessarily temporally (because causally) prior to the event referred to in the main clause. Thus the view of IF as essentially a modal particle signalling non-factivity which may have more specific meanings depending on its context of use seems to be appropriate for the description of IF in the language of children.

The use of questions to represent addressee-oriented modality, on the other hand, as discussed in 9.4, appears to be a somewhat later development in child language than the ontogenetically more fundamental use of eliciting a response from one's addressee, and thus Lyons' (1977: 754) characterization of interrogative sentences as 'the grammaticalisation of the feature of doubt' is appropriate only at a fairly high level of abstraction.[3] It has been frequently noted that 'caretaker' speech to young children makes more use of questions than any other type of utterance (cf. Savić, 1975) and references given in Keenan *et al.* (1978) suggest that the reason for this is that interrogative utterances in caretaker speech may be classified either as 'directives to attend' or as articulations of an immediate concern of the speaker—i.e. they are used primarily as a means of controlling the child's behaviour. Naturally enough, the child appears to use questions in the same way, and thus any analysis in terms of addressee-oriented modality would appear to be inappropriate in the early stages. Later on, however, when the child begins to use tag questions and indirect questions, a modality analysis is probably more justified.

In summary, although the evidence is insufficient to enable a detailed account of the development of the child's expression of modality up to the age of 5, there are a number of general observations which can be made.

Modality appears to be expressed first by means of past tense forms and the modals CAN and WILL, although these are used in a far more restricted way than in adult language. By the age of 5 most of the other modals are being used, but WILL and CAN are still the most frequent, and the secondary modals together with MAY and MUST are still comparatively rare. The quasi-auxiliary expressions HAVE(GOT)TO, BE GOING TO, and HAD BETTER are used quite frequently, as are tag questions and I THINK. Insufficient research has been done to enable us to estimate in any detail the extent to which the modal expressions of a 5-year-old are used in the same way that an adult would use them, but it seems likely that the secondary modals at least have not yet been fully mastered, and modal adverbs, objective modal expressions with BE (apart from BE GOING TO), and modal lexical verbs (apart from I THINK) appear to be used very little, if at all. In addition, tense (at least in the earlier stages) and IF-clauses are used in a rather more restricted way than in adult speech. Any overall assessment is further complicated by the fact that social background and general verbal ability clearly have some effect on the 5-year-old's expression of modality.

It is still possible, nevertheless, to suggest a number of hypotheses to account for the development of the expression of modality up to the age of 5, but before I go on to discuss these in 11.4 I will first examine the period between 6 and 12 years old, about which even less is known.

11.3 Modal expressions from 6 to 12

11.3.1 Review of the literature

Relatively little research has been carried out into the language development of children after the age of 5, largely because the average 5-year-old appears to be so proficient in saying what he wants to that he may give the impression of having little left to learn. However, the mere fact that cognitive development continues at least until puberty suggests that language development does not stand still after 5—and in fact there is now a significant body of research to back up this hypothesis. Estimates of exactly how much remains to be learned range from Carol Chomsky's (1969: 4) comparatively weak hypothesis that 'structures which have potential for late acquisition would be those, for example, which deviate from a widely established pattern in the language, or whose surface structure is relatively inexplicit with respect to grammatical relations, or even simply those which the linguist finds particularly difficult to incorporate into a thorough description', to Ingram's (1975: 103) comparatively strong hypothesis that 'between the ages of 5 or 6 and 12, the child restructures his grammar of English from a predominantly phrase structure grammar to a predominantly transformational one'. A number of studies (which are reviewed in Karmiloff-Smith, 1979) have followed Carol Chomsky's lead and examined the development of specific and often problematical elements in the language of over-5s, whereas a number of other studies—e.g. Loban (1961, 1966), Hunt (1964, 1965, 1970), O'Donnell et al. (1967), and Richardson et al. (1976) (none of which is referred to in Karmiloff-

Smith's review article)—have undertaken large scale studies of syntactic development which appear to strongly support Ingram's hypothesis. However, of all these studies the only ones to date to have cast more than a fleeting glance at modal expressions are Turner (1973) and Major (1974).

Turner is mainly concerned with the social determinants of children's language of control at ages 5 and 7, and although he distinguishes between use of 'imperative-type commands'—e.g.:

410 Go away.
411 You go away.

and 'obligation-type commands'—e.g.:

412 You must go away.
413 You'd better go away.

it is unclear from the way is data is presented (Turner, 1973: 169 f.) whether the latter type were used comparatively more or less frequently by the older children, and no details are given about what kinds of 'obligation-type commands' were actually used.

Major's study is somewhat more revealing, although it has limitations of a different kind. She tested 44 children between the age of 5 and 8 on their comprehension of, and manipulatory skills with, CAN, COULD, WILL, WOULD, SHALL, SHOULD, MAY, MIGHT, MUST, OUGHT TO, NEED, and DARE as well as HAD BETTER, WOULD RATHER, BE GOING TO, and HAVE TO, by getting the children to (a) imitate fifty sentences containing a modal and a main verb, a modal and a progressive form, or a modal and a perfective form; (b) convert nineteen affirmative sentences to negatives; and (c) supply tag questions for nineteen affirmative statements. Very broadly, her findings were that all the children were familiar with the expressions, but the older children coped better than the younger children with the imitation of the progressive and perfective auxiliary constructions and the transformation tasks. The overall order of difficulty of the tasks from less to more difficult was: (1) imitation of unexpanded modals; (2) imitation of modal progressives; (3) questions; (4) negations; (5) perfects; and (6) tags. Most children showed reasonable facility with CAN, COULD, WILL, WOULD, and SHOULD in most tasks, whereas general difficulty was experienced with MAY, MIGHT, SHALL, MUST, NEED, DARE, OUGHT TO, WOULD RATHER, and HAD BETTER in the negation, tag, and question transformation tasks.

This brief summary of Major's findings is sufficient to show that children of 8 have clearly not yet fully mastered the English modal system. However, it is not easy to draw any particular firm conclusions about modal usage in 5- to 8-year olds' language from Major's results because of one fundamental limitation in her study—namely, that she generally does not take into account the fact that the context of a modal will invariably affect the way its meaning is interpreted. Although she is very careful in her syntactic classification of the modals, her treatment of the semantics of the modals is less satisfactory. Fletcher (1975: 321) in his review of Major (1974) points to specific items where imitation problems may well have been due to the meaning of the modal in a particular context, rather than simply to the transformational complexity of the sentence. Another problem may also have been that the progressive and perfective sentences were nearly always longer than those with the unexpanded modal and therefore slightly more difficult to remember. Fletcher remarks that the only zero score on an imitation task was on one of the longest sentences in the list:

414 Sarah ought to have worn her mittens today.

Nevertheless, Major's study is still the only extensive analysis of the modals in the language of children over 5 to have been published so far, and it is therefore of considerable interest.

11.3.2 Analysis of data from the Polytechnic of Wales Language Development Project[4]

In order to supplement our meagre knowledge of the modal usage of children over the age of 5, I have carried out a study of the modal expressions used in the spontaneous speech of 96 children from 6 to 12 years old who participated in the Polytechnic of Wales Language Development Project, directed by Robin Fawcett. The project is an ongoing large-scale study of general syntactic and semantic development in 6- to 12-year-old children and should ultimately provide a fairly detailed picture of several aspects of language development in the primary school years. A preliminary report of the project has been published (Fawcett and Perkins, 1981) and the transcribed data with a preface have been published in four volumes (Fawcett and Perkins, 1980), which have been reviewed by Scott (1982).

The study of modal expressions was carried out on a sample made up of 32 groups of three children (see Table 11.3), in which each child was of the same age (i.e. within three months of his/her 6th, 8th, 10th, or 12th birthday), sex, and social background. All the children were monolingual English speakers and attended schools in the Pontypridd area of Mid Glamorgan, South Wales (see Wells

Table 11.3   Sample of children from the Polytechnic of Wales Language
Development Project used in the study of modal expressions

		6		8		10		12	
Age:									
Sex:		M	F	M	F	M	F	M	F
Social background:	A	3	3	3	3	3	3	3	3
	B	3	3	3	3	3	3	3	3
	C	3	3	3	3	3	3	3	3
	D	3	3	3	3	3	3	3	3

(1982, Vol. 2: 377 ff.) and Hughes and Trudgill (1979: 51 ff.) for accent and dialect characteristics of the area). In addition, the members of each group were judged by their teachers to be compatible in a play situation, and the teacher's experience was also drawn on to exclude any child who could be described as 'atypical' in any way (e.g. on the grounds of physical or mental disability, excessive tension at home, etc.). As shown in Table 11.3, for each of the age groups 6, 8, 10, and 12 there were eight cells (4 male and 4 female) of which two cells (1 male and 1 female) represented each of four different categories of social background: A (highest), B, C, and D.[5]

The data used for the purposes of the study of modal expressions consisted of stereophonic tape-recordings (to provide a three-dimensional signal) and transcriptions (carried out by trained transcribers) of ten minutes of spontaneous conversation from the members of each cell, who were recorded while engaged in building a house or some other construction of their own choosing out of Lego bricks. No other person was present in the room during the recording and the children on the whole appeared to feel themselves alone and unobserved.[5] Although the task in hand provided in all cases a clear point of focus for conversation, other conversational topics were also covered.

As most previous studies of modal expressions had concentrated almost exclusively on the modal auxiliaries, it was decided in this case to examine the usage not only of the expressions discussed in Chapter 3 but also of the majority of those discussed in Chapters 4 to 7. Expressions which were omitted from the study were modal lexical verbs used with a second- or third-person subject, and also the boulomaic modal verbs WANT TO and WISH, which were at the time considered to be of less central interest. Tense, IF-clauses, and questions were taken into consideration only if a modal expression was involved. Any repetition of an expression due to hesitancy was not counted.

11.3.3 *General results*

The frequency of usage of each modal expression for the whole sample is shown in Table 11.4. One fact which may at first be surprising is that the range of expressions used is so restricted. Expressions other than the modal auxiliaries and a limited number of quasi-auxiliaries are hardly in evidence at all. This does not mean, of course, that such expressions are not understood and never used by the children in the sample, but simply that they were not used in the interactions which were recorded. Some suggestions as to why this should be so will be put forward later, but we can make the anticipatory comment that presumably the children only used those expressions which they felt were necessary to get across the meanings they wished to express, and the expressions they did use were thought to be adequate in the particular situation in which they were involved.

The second interesting point is that Table 11.4 bears a striking resemblance to Table 11.2 which reports the findings of Wells (1979) for the spontaneous speech of much younger children—i.e. up to the age of 3;6. This is probably no coincidence, since Wells (1979: 262) notes that the distribution of modal expressions in the speech addressed by adults to the children in his sample closely parallels that of the children's speech, and 'it is just those forms that figure most frequently in the adults' speech that are acquired first and used most frequently by the children'. Whether or not the distribution of modal expressions in inter-adult speech is the same as in adult–child speech is not clear, but the fact that the speech of 6- to 12-year-old children to one another manifests a similar distribution suggests that at least for informal situations of this kind, the range and relative frequency of modal expressions used may well differ little for children and adults.[6]

Figure 11.1[7] shows how frequency of use of modal expressions varies in relation to the sex, socio-economic background, and age of the users. Sex appears to have comparatively little effect on the overall frequency of usage of modal expressions (but see comments below on I THINK and SHOULD), and since similar results are obtained when most modal expressions are considered individually, the variable of sex will be largely ignored from now on. Age and social background, on the other hand, do seem to have a significant effect. It appears that children from a more favoured social background use modal expressions more frequently than children from a less favoured social background. The effect of age on frequency is more difficult to interpret. Although there is a clear correlation

Table 11.4   Order of frequency of modal expressions in the spontaneous speech of 6- to 12-year-old children

	Total number of occurrences	Percentage of overall total
CAN	473	25.9
WILL	420	23.0
HAVE(GOT)TO	255	14.0
BE GOING TO	187	10.2
COULD	95	5.2
WOULD	80	4.4
I THINK	74	4.1
SHALL	54	3.0
SHOULD	47	2.6
BE SUPPOSED TO	31	1.7
MIGHT	25	1.4
MUST	21	1.2
HAD BETTER	14	0.8
PROBABLY	8	0.4
BE ABLE TO	6	0.3
BE ALLOWED TO	5	0.3
MAY	5	0.3
NEED TO	5	0.3
I EXPECT	4	0.2
I SUPPOSE	4	0.2
MAYBE	3	0.2
I RECKON	3	0.2
DARE	2	0.1
OUGHT TO	2	0.1
PERHAPS	2	0.1
I HAVE A FEELING THAT	1	0.1

between age and frequency of use of modal expressions between the ages of 6 and 10, the data suggests that after 10 this frequency decreases rather sharply. Why this should be so is not at all clear. Ideally one might have expected frequency of usage to increase gradually to some level which was thereafter maintained. It seems unlikely that the 12-year-olds' mastery of modal expressions is less developed than that of the 10-year-olds. Perhaps even more surprising is the fact (not shown in Figure 11.1) that within the 12-year-old sample it is the children from the *highest* socio-economic group who use modal expressions *least* frequently (18.7 per cent of the total compared with 28.6 per cent for group B, 27.0 per cent for group C, and 25.7 per cent for group D). Clearly, some further factor is involved which has not been taken into account, but the findings reported so far do not suggest any obvious solution to the problem. However, in 11.4 where a number

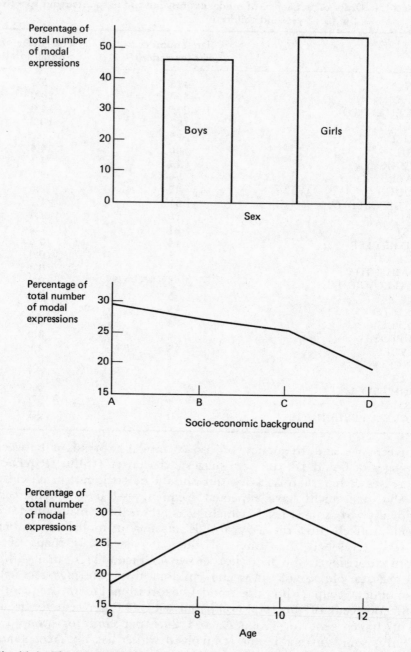

Fig. 11.1 The relation of frequency of modal expressions to sex, age, and socio-economic background

of non-linguistic factors are taken into consideration, a possible explanation will be proposed.

Before going on to a more detailed look at the results obtained, I would like to make clear the inherent limitations of the data and of the conclusions which may be inferred from them. It must be remembered that the situation in which the data were produced is not representative of the entire spectrum of human interaction. In all cases the conversation was between three friends involved in a common task and was therefore bound to be very informal. Also, although the conversation often touched on a number of different topics, it was inevitably anchored to the task of building something with Lego bricks. A further consideration to note is that some children tend to be more talkative than others, and the less talkative will therefore be less well represented in the data.

Given these limitations, however, it is still felt that the sample is large enough, and the situation representative enough of much human interaction, to ensure that the observations made are of considerable generality.

11.3.4 CAN

The frequency distribution of CAN relative to age is given in Figure 11.2. The slightly higher incidence of CAN at age 6 than at ages 8, 10, and 12 is a reflection of the fact that CAN counted for as much as 39.5 per cent of the total usage of modal expressions for the 6-year-olds (as much as 65.0 per cent and 57.1 per cent for 6CB[8] and 6DB respectively), whereas this reduced to 23.4 per cent at age 12. Simple frequency counts do not give the whole picture, however, unless sentential environment and meaning are taken into account as well. Although CAN was used with a similar degree of frequency in negative and interrogative environments in all four age groups, it was used more frequently with a first person singular subject at age 6 than at any other age, and there appears to be a clear

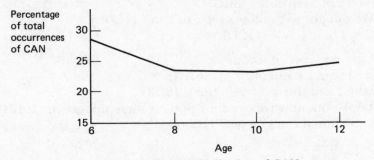

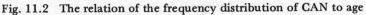

Fig. 11.2 The relation of the frequency distribution of CAN to age

correlation between age and the percentage of instances of CAN
used with a first person plural subject, as shown in Table 11.5.

Table 11.5 Distribution of CAN with singular and plural first person subjects
at ages 6, 8, 10, and 12.

Age	Percentage of uses of CAN with I as subject	Percentage of uses of CAN with WE as subject
6	37.1	9.6
8	22.5	22.5
10	32.7	24.6
12	19.7	33.3

In order to see whether there was any difference in the way children of different ages used CAN, each instance was classified according to whether (a) K = natural laws/C = empirical circumstances
originating within the subject of the sentence (glossed as 'ability');
(b) K = social laws/C = a deontic source (glossed as 'permission');
(c) K = natural laws/C = empirical circumstances external to the
subject of the sentence (glossed as 'circumstantial possibility');
(d) K = natural laws/C = empirical circumstances, where the utterance
has the illocutionary force of a suggestion (i.e. what Shields (1974:
191) has called 'role' and 'rule' meanings) (glossed as 'suggestion').
Some examples of these four categories are:

a. *Ability*:
415 I can make settees, I can. (6AB)
416 I can't undo it. (8CG)
417 I can't get the Lego to fit together. (10BG)
418 Can't stand building this. (12DB).

b. *Permission*:
419 Can I have one of them? (6BG)
420 You can have mine. (8CG)
421 We can put any colours on, can't we? (10DB)
422 Can I have a few? (12DB)

c. *Circumstantial possibility*:
423 What can I stand mine in? (6AG)
424 Where can this ladder go then? (8CB)
425 Look, um, now we can start putting these things on. (10BB)
426 How stupid can you get? (12BG)

d. *Suggestion*:
427 That can be a bus station. (6BB)

428 This can be the park-keeper. (8AG)
429 I'll tell you what—you can put that on top of there. (10DG)

When the uses of CAN in the data are classified in this way, the picture shown in Table 11.6 emerges. Before any inferences are made, however, a severe note of caution should be sounded. In many cases it is difficult, if not impossible, to say categorically that one, and only one, of these four meanings is intended. There are two reasons for this. Firstly, in order to interpret an utterance containing CAN, one must assign a definite value to the C variable—usually on the basis of contextual clues, and often there is insufficient evidence to decide. For example, in the following:

430 The traffic can travel all around it, can't it? (6BG)

we may guess that 'ability' is probably not intended, since traffic is non-animate (although, of course, this is not necessarily the child's view) and the tag seems to rule out a 'permission' sense. It is not at all clear, however, whether the child is making a suggestion or merely stating a circumstantial possibility. Sometimes uncertainty in such cases is due to the fact that there is limited contextual information available on the tape recording, but this is not always so.

The second point, which follows on from the first, is that one is not always justified in setting up such a semantic grid to analyse these kinds of data. The four semantic glosses refer to objectified notions, whereas CAN expresses a meaning which is not inherently objective (cf. 5.1) and it may well be that CAN is sometimes used with the precise intention of not committing the speaker to one or another of these explicit objective notions. And, more germane to the present context, one cannot be sure without carrying out comprehension tests whether a given child is yet aware that CAN may have these four different connotations. On rare occasions the child makes clear the precise sense in which a sentence with CAN is to be understood, as in the following examples:

431 Oh, I can make—I know how to make the telephone boxes. (10AB)
432 But we can't put cars on it, can we? Are we allowed to put cars on it? (6DB)

In (431) CAN is rejected, since it is not sufficiently explicit to convey the exact meaning intended, and in (432) CAN is replaced by BE ALLOWED TO in order to make the meaning clearer.

In most cases, however, CAN is left to stand by itself and it is not

Table 11.6 Uses of CAN at ages 6, 8, 10, and 12 classified according to meaning

Age	'Ability'	'Permission'	'Circumstantial possibility'	'Suggestion'
6	30.4%	38.5%	21.5%	9.6%
8	33.3%	6.3%	39.6%	20.7%
10	32.7%	15.5%	40.0%	11.8%
12	25.6%	3.4%	56.4%	14.5%

always unreasonable to assume that its precise meaning in such cases is nothing more nor less than 'can'. I shall return to this discussion in 11.3.9—the reason for bringing it up now is to make the point that although the figures in Table 11.6 might appear to suggest that the use of CAN to express 'circumstantial possibility' becomes more frequent as the child grows older, and that the use of CAN to make 'suggestions' is more frequent after the age of 6, some of the decisions from which the figures are calculated were made on the basis of insufficient evidence, and some interpretations may credit the child with a more explicit meaning than he/she intended.

11.3.5 WILL

In the use of WILL the most notable correlation is between frequency and social background, as shown in Figure 11.3.

At 6 years old, WILL acounts for only 15.5 per cent of the total modal output, but this percentage increases to 24.5 per cent at age 8, and this appears to remain more or less constant (i.e. 25.6 per cent at age 10 and 23.0 per cent at age 12). As is the case with CAN, first person singular subjects are far more frequent than second

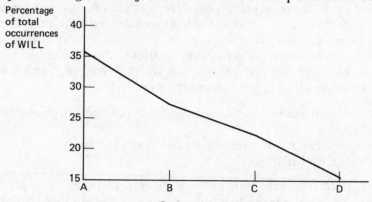

Fig. 11.3 The relation of the frequency distribution of WILL to socio-economic background

person subjects at age 6, and this is reversed from 8 onwards. Over 75 per cent of the time WILL was realized as 'LL, the majority of the remaining 25 per cent of instances being in negative and interrogative environments.

11.3.6 HAVE(GOT)TO

Like WILL, HAVE(GOT)TO becomes relatively more frequent after the age of 6 and there is a notable decrease in its use with first person singular subjects (30.2 per cent at age 6, 20.6 per cent at age 8, 21.1 per cent at age 10, and 12.3 per cent at age 12). It was usually always restricted to occurrence with WILL, which accounted for approximately 25 per cent of instances.

11.3.7 BE GOING TO

The frequency of BE GOING TO does not significantly increase with age, although the way it is used appears to change, as can be seen from Table 11.7. The use of BE GOING TO with first person singular subjects decreases as its use with first person plural subjects increases, and its use in complex sentences—and in particular in WH-questions —also increases with age. (Cf. Ingram's (1975: 103) hypothesis cited in 11.3.1.)

11.3.8 Other modal expressions

The less frequent modal expressions can be dealt with more briefly. COULD was used very little by the 6-year-olds and not at all with a first person plural subject. With the 8-, 10-, and 12-year olds, on the other hand, 48.7 per cent, 38.1 per cent, and 42.3 per cent of occurrences respectively had WE as subject.

WOULD differed from most other modal expressions in that it was used predominantly with third person subjects at all ages (i.e. 60 per cent at age 6, 42.9 per cent at age 8, 60.5 per cent at age 10, and 53.9 per cent at age 12).

I THINK was one of the two expressions (cf. SHOULD below) to be used by significantly more girls (61.3%) than boys (38.7%) and since its primary function (probably more so than most other modal expressions in the data—cf. Chapter 7 and note 5 in that chapter) appears to be to express simple subjective uncertainty or politeness/ deference, this would seem to be compatible with Klann–Delius' (1981) hypothesis that sex differences in language learning are largely restricted to the 'pragmatic–semantic' domain, and to offer some support for the thesis of Lakoff (1975) and others who hold that girls are brought up to conform to the stereotypical ideal of woman as unassertive and lacking in confidence.

Table 11.7   The change in use of BE GOING TO between the ages of 6 and 12

Age	I-Subject	We-Subject	WH-Questions	Simple sentences
6	60.5%	5.3%	5.3%	18.4%
8	45.5%	11.4%	11.4%	25.0%
10	26.5%	10.2%	10.2%	24.5%
12	16.1%	35.7%	23.2%	46.4%

There were only two instances of SHALL in the speech of the 6-year-olds, and every use of SHALL at all ages was always in a first person subject interrogative environment.

Only 10.6 per cent of the occurrences of SHOULD were clearly epistemic, and this was the only other expression apart from I THINK to be used mainly by girls (i.e. 63.8 per cent vs. 36.1 per cent for the boys).

Of the other expressions, MIGHT and MAY were always used epistemically, except in the formulaic expression MIGHT AS WELL and MAY AS WELL, and MUST was used deontically more than 75 per cent of the time. The majority of modal expressions were used too rarely for frequency ratings to provide much insight, but it is perhaps significant that BE ABLE TO, DARE (which was used only in the formulaic expression I DARE SAY), I EXPECT, I HAVE A FEELING, MAY, OUGHT TO, PERHAPS, PROBABLY, I RECKON, and I SUPPOSE were not used at all by the 6-year-olds.

11.3.9 Further points of interest

It is a major drawback of data of the kind presented here that it provides evidence only of what a child actually said, as opposed to what he might have said had he wanted or if circumstances had been otherwise, and it also reveals only a limited amount of what the child is capable of understanding. However, as Karmiloff-Smith (1979: 322) has noted: 'Whilst the over 5 year old's language is often super-ficially correct, important clues to ongoing development can be gleaned from children's hesitations and spontaneous corrections' and there are one or two sequences in the data which are rather suggestive in this respect.

It is perhaps significant, as will be seen presently, that HAVE (GOT)TO is used so much more frequently than MUST. MUST is used, but nearly 70 per cent of its occurrences appear in the 6-year-olds' speech, and are, furthermore, confined to the speech of two girls in particular; but interestingly, both these girls seem to be following different strategies with regard to the use of MUST. The one girl, K, uses MUST only in the negative—cf:

433 K: Oh you *mustn't* have two colours, 'cos they both gotta be
the same colour, *mustn't* they? (6AG)
434 S: There's gotta be a door upstairs 'cos . . .
K: There *mustn't*. (6AG)

Here, MUST is clearly being used as a, suppletive form of HAVE
(GOT)TO which, when negated, typically has the meaning 'not
necessary that p' as opposed to 'necessary that not-p'. Although
K uses HAVE(GOT)TO a number of times, it is never used in the
negative, for which purposes MUST appears to be reserved.

The other girl, C, on the other hand, appears to use MUST as a
performative suppletive of HAVE(GOT)TO—i.e. it is always used
in directives with a second person subject, as in:

435 No, you *must* get your own. (6BG)
436 You *must* share. (6BG)
437 But you *must* have room for this. (6BG)
438 You *must* move it over so the bus can go in there. (6BG)
439 You *mustn't* have it all to yourself. (6BG)

HAVE(GOT)TO is used by C in a non-performative sense with first
and third person subjects, as in:

440 I *have to* take a black. (6BG)
441 He *gotta* be like that because he's sitting down. (6BG)

This restricted use of MUST is possible evidence that these two
girls are not yet fully aware of the precise place and function of
MUST in the adult linguistic system, and are still testing out their
own hypotheses as to how MUST is to be used. Each girl's use of
MUST is by no means abnormal in itself—i.e. it is syntactically and
semantically appropriate—and yet the fact that it is used in such a
limited way and, apart from the speech of these two girls, is hardly
used at all in the data seems to suggest that the two girls in question
are somewhat atypical.

There is some evidence that certain modal expressions are seen by
some children as being semantically equivalent—or at least less
different than one might have predicted—as in the following:

442 There ought to be a little window by here, shouldn't there?
(12CG)
443 Somebody might think that's a bit of the house as well, wouldn't
they? (10AG)
444 We're going to start (treating?) things now, won't we? (10DG)

Although the tag is not formally related to the main clause in (442),

(443), and (444), it is clearly felt by the children that there is some semantic link. (442) would be entirely acceptable to some adults as well (cf. 3.4), and it is also possible that (443) and (444) might pass unnoticed in an adult conversation—but in the latter two cases it is possible that it would be put down to a slip of the tongue. This may, of course, also be the case in the children's speech, although it is impossible to tell. Certainly, one child at least does not regard WILL and BE GOING TO as being semantically equivalent, as is shown in the following example:

445 He's gonna—he'll tell us to be quiet. (12CG)

where BE GOING TO would perhaps have expressed a greater degree of certainty than the child felt. Further research would need to be done, however, in order to find out whether children actually do regard OUGHT TO and SHOULD, MIGHT and WOULD, and WILL and BE GOING TO as being semantically equivalent.

One further way of gaining insight into children's passive knowledge of language is to look for examples where a child reveals discomfort with the way something has been expressed. In the following, for example:

446 M: We'll just have to not do it.
    P: We won't have to do it. (6BB)

immediately P appears to convert, or 'correct', what M has said into a more amenable form.

Examples of possible discrepancies in comprehension such as those noted here are extremely rare, however, and for the most part the children studied seem quite competent at expressing what they mean. And yet the fact that the results of Major (1974) discussed above have shown that children over the age of 6 may not yet be fully conversant with the subtleties of the way modality is expressed in English suggests that the children in the present study only use expressions which they are reasonably sure of; and, in fact, the expressions which Major found caused some difficulty for 5- to 8-year-olds in negation, tag, and question transformation tasks appear comparatively rarely in the Polytechnic of Wales data.

To the general strategy of only using expressions of which one is reasonably sure may also be added the principle that one should never be more explicit than one needs to be. This may appear rather obvious, but it affords a way of explaining why the range of modal expressions used in the data is so restricted. Judging from the data, the core of the English modal system would appear to be the modal auxiliaries and quasi-auxiliaries, and in particular CAN, WILL, and

HAVE(GOT)TO. According to the analysis proposed in Chapters 3 to 8, these two categories constitute the least objective set of modal expressions (CAN and WILL in particular being the only modal auxiliaries which may be subject oriented) and there is ample evidence in the data (as I have already noted in the discussion of CAN in 11.3.4) that the more formally explicit forms are used only in cases where a less explicit form would have been too vague. For example, the following extracts contain the only uses of BE ABLE TO in the data:

447 We wouldn't be able to play with them properly. (8AG)
448 We won't be able to play with them. (8AG)
449 At the front I won't be able to put it. (8AG)
450 We won't be able to do them all the same colours. (8CB)
451 We won't be able to do another layer though, will we? (10BB)
452 You won't be able to open the doors if you have that. (12DB)

and it is highly significant that in every case CAN could not have been used, since it cannot occur with WILL or WOULD. This lends considerable psychological respectability to the grammatical notion of 'suppletive form'—which BE ABLE TO clearly is here—i.e. it is a form which one uses only when there is no way of avoiding it. Interestingly, however, from the limited evidence present in the data, it would appear more reasonable to regard MUST as a suppletive of HAVE(GOT)TO rather than the other way round as many grammatical analyses would predict, since the former hardly ever occurs in the data, whereas the latter is the third most frequent modal expression.

Although there is much that we still do not know about the development of modal expressions, the information presented above is sufficient to indicate several significant developmental trends which any theory of language development must attempt to explain. In 11.4 I will briefly discuss one or two hypotheses from the child development literature which may go some way towards explaining some of the trends noted above, and I will also assess the extent to which the framework for the analysis of modal expressions proposed in Chapters 3 to 8 constitutes a suitable format for analysing the development of modal expressions.

11.4 Towards a theory of the development of modal expressions

It was argued in Chapters 3 to 8 that the use and comprehension of modal expressions is dependent upon specific types of knowledge of the world, and it was thus suggested at the beginning of this chapter that since the way children comprehend the world changes as they grow older, it should also follow that their usage and comprehension of modal expressions will change. However, although we have indeed seen that a number of systematic changes in the way children express modality do in fact occur as they grow older, we may not necessarily assume that *all* such changes are a direct consequence of the child's cognitive development. Although it is now generally accepted that linguistic development and cognitive development are significantly related, other factors such as syntactic complexity (cf. Slobin, 1973) and pragmatic considerations (cf., for example, Bates (1976), Bruner (1978), Waterson and Snow (1978), and Wells (1981)) also play a part. Syntax and pragmatics, however, present difficulties when used as frameworks for the analysis of linguistic development. In the former case, any scale of syntactic complexity will be largely defined by the particular theory of syntax one is using, and what the theory predicts as being complex will not necessarily coincide with what is psychologically complex. The dangers of using syntactic complexity as a developmental yardstick are exemplified in the fact that only a year after the publication of a paper (Brown and Hanlon, 1970) which appeared to confirm the ontogenetic version of the derivational complexity hypothesis (namely that the number of grammatical transformations needed in the derivation of a given structure is directly related to the stage at which such a structure is mastered by the child), Brown (1970: 156) saw fit to point out that 'with more knowledge of the facts of acquisition, I find that I can make quite a long list of exceptions to the rule'. (Cf. also Bresnan, 1978.)

The problem with trying to use pragmatic complexity to predict the course of linguistic development is that no sufficiently detailed theory of linguistic interaction exists, and although a considerable amount of research has been carried out on caretaker–child interaction as a determinant of linguistic development (see Wells and Robinson (1982) for a recent review) such work is still in its infancy.

Cognitive development, on the other hand, has the advantage of having been formulated within an illuminating, if not entirely empirically adequate (cf., for example, Donaldson, 1978 and Boden, 1979), theoretical framework—namely that of Piaget. Although Piaget's theory is not the only theory of cognitive development (cf. Turner, 1975: 28 ff.), it is certainly the best known and the most widely researched, and has already proved a rich source of hypotheses for a number of otherwise inexplicable features of language development (cf., for example, Bloom (1973), Cromer (1970), Sinclair–de Zwart (1973) and Cambon and Sinclair (1974)). In addition,

Piaget's theory also embraces the development of moral judgement (Piaget, 1932), which is particularly relevant to deontic modality (cf. Tomlinson, 1980: 331: 'Morality is essentially about judgement concerning obligation—moral principles the basis for resolving conflicts of obligation'), and the development of rational thought (e.g. Piaget, 1926, and Piaget and Inhelder, 1958), which is relevant to epistemic modality. Although Piaget's theory of developmental stages can be criticized on points of detail (Donaldson (1978), for example, cites experimental evidence which shows that Piaget has sometimes tended to underestimate children's powers of reason), and in general on account of its vagueness (cf. Boden, 1979: 153), it still provides a convenient and illuminating model of many of the changes which can be seen to occur between infancy and adulthood.

In this section, therefore, I shall try to account for some of the observations made in 11.2 and 11.3 within a broadly Piagetian framework, while recognizing that such a framework does not enable us to give the complete picture. The stages of cognitive development proposed by Piaget are so well known that I will merely refer the reader to Piaget (1970) and Boden (1979) for an account of them.

Modal expressions are first used at the beginning of the pre-operational period, which is the period associated with egocentrism. As Turner (1975: 19) puts it: 'this egocentric attitude is really a particular example of a more general characteristic and that is the preoperational child's inability to consider two aspects of the same situation at one and the same time: he will consider one, for example, to the exclusion of all other relevant information'. For some time the only modal expressions used are usually CAN and WILL, and it is interesting that not only are these the only modal auxiliaries which may be subject oriented (cf. 3.3.2) but, as Fletcher (1979: 281) points out, this is the only sense in which they appear to be used by the 2-year-old: he uses CAN and WILL either 'for himself (to indicate willingness, inability, or request for permission), or to allow or prohibit an action by his addressee. He does not use modals to refer to the willingness or ability of third persons'. It will be recalled that even at the age of 6, WILL and CAN were used predominantly with a first person singular subject, and that the proportion of first person singular subjects declined dramatically in the speech of 8-, 10-, and 12-year olds—i.e. after the preoperational period.

Egocentrism may also account for the fact that MUST and MAY, which are not generally subject oriented, are so rarely used in young children's speech, since they are essentially 'linguistic devices "displaced" from the events to which they refer' (Fletcher, 1979: 283).

The dramatic change from the use of I to the use of WE as the most frequent subject of modal expressions in the speech of 8-, 10-, and 12-year-olds is probably related to the development of the child's attitude towards rules. When Piaget (1932)[9] studied the way children understood and applied the rules of the game of marbles, he found that children between the ages of 3 and 7 (i.e. the preoperational period) simply imitated other children. As he puts it: 'though he imitates what he observes, and believes in perfect good faith that he is playing like the others, the child thinks nothing at first but of utilising these new acquisitions for himself. He plays in an individualistic manner with material that is social. Such is egocentrism'. After the age of 7, however, begins what Piaget calls a stage of 'incipient cooperation' which coincides with the concrete operational period, and during which children play according to mutually agreed rules. Since modal expressions are probably the primary linguistic means for talking about and establishing rules and social constraints, it seems quite natural that a change from an individualistic to a cooperative attitude towards rules should be reflected in the type of subject used with modal expressions. The fact that the data discussed in 11.3 were recorded in a situation where the children were involved in a common task for which it was necessary to establish a method of procedure was bound to accentuate this difference.

Finally, round about the age of 11, a further stage occurs which Piaget calls the 'codification of rules' (coinciding with the formal operational period) in which 'not only is every detail of procedure in the game fixed, but the actual code of rules to be observed is known to the whole society. There is a remarkable concordance in the information given by children of 10–12 belonging to the same class at school, when they are questioned on the rules of the game and their possible variations'.

Although it is offered here only as a speculation, it is just possible that the reason for the decrease in the overall frequency of modal expressions in the data collected from the 12-year-old group, as discussed in 11.3.3, as compared with the 10- and 8-year-olds, is that the 12-year-olds (and in particular the most socially advantaged), presumably at the 'codification' stage, were more aware of the rules of social cooperation for a task such as that in which they were involved, and felt less need of discussing and establishing new cooperative rules.

Despite the apparent relevance of Piaget's theory of stages to the above linguistic phenomena, there remain a number of factors which it is not able to account for—at least on its own. Why is it, for example, that past tense forms appear later with modal auxiliary verbs than they do with regular main verbs? And why is it that modal adverbs, adjectival, participial, and nominal modal expressions are virtually non-existent in the data discussed in 11.3? If we are to account for these facts within a Piagetian framework we will need a linguistic description of modal expressions which can make relevant distinctions between the above-mentioned linguistic categories. The analytical framework established in Chapters 3 to 8 does, in fact, seem to go some way towards this.

It was argued in 3.4 that the secondary modal auxiliaries were 'doubly modal' in that they invoke not only a C variable, but also a further conditional variable Z to which the proposition or event is relativized. The past tense form of a non-modal verb, on the other hand, has only one degree of modality, due to the conditional variable indicated by the tense form. Interestingly, regular past tense forms of ordinary verbs appear round about the same time as CAN and WILL, which suggests a possibly common cognitive prerequisite. Although children are apparently unable to decenter in time until the age of about 4 years and 6 months (Cromer, 1971)[10]—which presumably means that any past tense forms used before this cannot refer to past time—Kuczaj and Daly (1979: 565) report evidence of hypothetical reference as early as 2 and 3. If this observation is accurate, then it lends support to the hypothesis of Antinucci and Miller (1976) to the effect that the 'past' tense is first used to convey non-actuality and that past time reference is a later and more specific use of the past tense form, and it also favours the analysis of secondary modal auxiliaries as expressing two degrees of modality.

In Chapters 5 to 8 it was proposed that modal adverbs and modal adjectival, participial, and nominal expressions be regarded as objectifications of the kind of modal relations expressed by modal auxiliary verbs. Notions such as 'possibility', as referred to in expressions like POSSIBLY, IT'S POSSIBLE THAT, and THERE'S A POSSIBILITY THAT, are of a far higher level of abstraction than the notion of an event being relative to a circumstance—as expressed by CAN. (The fact that CAN itself cannot be nominalized may be seen as additional evidence for this.) In view of this, one would expect such objective expressions not to be fully understood until the formal operations period—i.e. from about the age of 11—and it seems likely that it is only at this stage that a full appreciation of the concept of modality becomes possible. As Boden (1979: 67) puts it: 'Initially . . . the developing operations are tied to practical, concrete situations: hence the term *concrete* operational knowledge (seven to eleven). The present and actual is well understood at this age, and the possible can be glimpsed as a practicable extension of it. But the possible is not fully appreciated until adolescence (eleven to fifteen) when *formal* operational thinking enables the abstract (propositional) representation of alternative hypotheses and their deductive implications. The possible is now seen not as a mere might-have-been (or might-have-done), but as the general structural limits within which the actual must necessarily be situated.' The progression from the kind of meaning possible with a modal auxiliary to that possible with a modal nominal expression closely parallels the child's changing cognitive capacity between the concrete operational period and the formal operational period.

The fact that expressions such as POSSIBLY, ITS'S POSSIBLE THAT, and THERE'S A POSSIBILITY THAT are far from common in the sample of 12-year-old speech discussed above does not necessarily count against this view, since the data consisted only of highly informal conversation and one does not expect the expression of abstract ideas under such circumstances. As Lyons (1977: 845) notes: '[it] may well be that the objectification of epistemic necessity and possibility is a rather sophisticated and impersonal process which plays little part in ordinary non-scientific discourse'; and later (p. 849): 'the objectification of both epistemic and deontic modality is something we have here taken to be secondary in the acquisition of language'. The fact that the framework proposed in Chapters 3 to 8 can systematically relate such notions of subjectivity and objectivity to distinctions at the level of linguistic form thus makes it a suitable tool for the analysis of language development.

In the case of modal lexical verbs, however, which, apart from I THINK, are extremely rare in the data for 6- to 12-year-olds, some other kind of explanation must be sought, since in their first person singular form, they are obviously subjective. As noted in Chapter 7, by using a modal lexical verb such as ORDER, ASSERT, CLAIM, etc., the speaker assigns himself a highly specific role within a particular social system, and the rarity of such forms in the language of children of 12 and under is explicable on the grounds that firstly, a child is unlikely to have attained a level of sophistication sufficient for the use of such forms, and secondly, even if he had somehow acquired such knowledge, he would be unlikely to find himself in a situation where such forms were appropriate, except, perhaps, for the purposes of a game.

The only epistemic modal lexical verbs which occurred in the 6- to 12-year-old data were THINK, EXPECT, RECKON, and SUPPOSE —which are all fairly informal expressions of uncertainty. The use of verbs like INFER, HYPOTHESIZE, DEDUCE, etc., would presuppose a considerably sophisticated knowledge of human reasoning processes, which are such as would be found only at an advanced stage in the formal operational period.

Although various details of the development of modal expressions as reported in 11.2 and 11.3 still await an explanation, the combination of a core-meaning analysis together with a Piagetian developmental framework helps to explain some of the more salient trends. Such a perspective suggests that basic modal concepts such as non-actuality and relativization are grasped fairly early on by the preoperational child, but are restricted within an egocentric framework, as is apparent in the young child's use of CAN and WILL. The secondary modal auxiliaries, which require a grasp of the notion of double relativization, and MUST and MAY which, in their deontic sense at least, require an awareness of an often non-current and non-subjective deontic source, are a later development. The range of uses each modal expression will have in a particular child's repertoire will change and increase as his understanding of natural laws, of socially defined role-relationships and constraints and of rational thought matures, but it seems likely that complete mastery of the more purely objective range of modal expressions such as modal adverbs and adjectival, participial, and nominal modal expressions must wait until the child has attained a formal operational mode of thinking.

In order to fill in the details of this broad theoretical framework a great deal more must be found out about the way in which various types of modal expression are understood by children at different levels of development—particularly children over 5—and how they are used in a varied range of contexts; and it may be that further evidence will reveal serious inadequacies in the framework that has been proposed, but for present purposes it is enough that the nature of the development of modal expressions has been clarified to the point where several new testable hypotheses may be formulated.

Notes

1. The use of COULD is rare with children at this stage of development. In the case of Susan it seems to have been used *simply* as a formula in polite requests. W. R. Miller (1973: 382 f.) states: 'Susan said "Could I have a dish" or "Could you make this one" where other children would have said "I want a dish" or "Make this one". In the non-interrogative contexts its use was extremely rare.'
2. Bouma (1975: 319) refers to a study (Ramge, 1973) which shows *WILL* and *KANN* to be the first modals to be used productively by German children.
3. Lyons (1977: 800) does not back up his claim that subjectively modalized utterances and questions 'may well originate, ontogenetically, in the same psychological state of doubt' with any data or experimental evidence.

4. A greatly abridged version of this section was published as Perkins (1981).
5. For further details see Fawcett and Perkins (1980, 1981).
6. The frequency count of modal verbs in Coates (1983: Ch. 3) differs somewhat from that in Table 11.4—notably as regards the low frequency of HAVE(GOT)TO—but this is based on data of which only a small proportion (apparently less than 25 per cent) consisted of informal conversation between adults.
7. For a more detailed numerical breakdown see Perkins (1980).
8. The number refers to age, the first letter to social background (A, B, C, or D) and the second letter to sex (B for boys, G for girls).
9. Despite the fact that it was first published over fifty years ago, Piaget's *The Moral Judgement of the Child* is still only marginally dated, as is evident from recent reviews of the literature on the development of moral judgement such as Tomlinson (1980) and Weinreich-Haste (1979).
10. See Smith (1980) for a different view.

12   Conclusions and Implications

In order to establish a coherent framework for the discussion of modality, it has been necessary to distinguish between modality (a) as a philosophical concept, (b) as a semantic relationship between propositions/events, circumstances, and sets of laws, and (c) as the realization of such relationships at the level of linguistic form. (a) is largely the concern of the philosophy of mind; logicians are primarily interested in (b), and linguists in (c), whereas logical semanticists and linguistic semanticists meet somewhere between (b) and (c), coming from different directions. There is indeed much in common between these three different approaches, but because of the tendency of different disciplines to prefer their own mode of enquiry, many of the similarities have not been clearly signposted and some have been hardly recognized at all, which has meant that a number of dark areas have been left unexplored and that a number of questions to which this study has addressed itself, had not previously been asked —except, perhaps, on a note of whimsical speculation.

The approach adopted here has made it possible to throw some light on several specific issues. It was noted in 2.3, for example, that the interest of linguists in modality has rarely extended much beyond the modal auxiliary verbs, largely because this is effectively the only class of modal expressions in English that is syntactically distinct from all other expressions. Because of this, virtually all other modal expressions have been ignored in linguistic studies (apart from an eclectic interest in 'quasi-auxiliary' modal expressions and the occasional discussion of modal adverbs), or else brought in only as supposedly synonymous paraphrases of the modals. However, we have seen that no two modal expressions are exact synonyms, and that the same types of semantic considerations which are reflected in the syntactic properties of the modals also appear to underlie the defining syntactic characteristics of non-auxiliary modal expressions. The provision of a semantic definition of the term 'modal expression' has made it possible to systematize what was previously regarded as a rather heterogeneous assortment of largely unrelated expressions, and the analysis of non-auxiliary modal expressions in Chapters 4 to 8 plugs a rather large gap in currently available descriptions of English. The semantic framework, further-more, also enables us to explain the 'centrality' of the modals in English.

Before proceeding any further, it is worth pausing to consider the theoretical and methodological implications of the points noted in the preceding paragraph. First of all, it seems clear that the technique of semantic analysis by paraphrase (notwithstanding its undoubted value) should perhaps be used with rather more circum-spection than is often the case. We have seen, for example, in 3.3.4 that judgements about negated WILL are sometimes based solely on observations of the effect of negation on BE PROBABLE THAT, under the mistaken assumption that the two expressions are synonyms. The means of showing lack of synonymy proposed here —namely, the comparison of two expressions in terms of their relative formal explicitness—provides a useful check on intuitive judgements of synonymy and might usefully be applied as an analy-tical parameter in other areas of linguistics. I have noted in 5.6, for example, that Ross's performative analysis of sentences fails principally because he does not take into account the dimension of formal explicitness.

A second point is that the core-meaning approach which is used in Chapters 3 to 8 appears to offer some confirmation of Bolinger's thesis (1977) of 'one form one meaning'—regarded as heretical, at least according to transformational dogma (cf. Geis, 1979). This type of approach goes hand in hand with a particular view of syntax which will have been apparent throughout this study—namely that syntax is as it is primarily by virtue of the semantic and pragmatic constraints upon individual expressions. As a practical principle, this may not always work, but in the case of the modal expressions examined above it appears to be amply borne out. The fact that many of the formal distinctions between different categories of modal expressions coincide with different degrees of politeness that the expressions may be used to convey (as shown in Chapter 10) also lends support to this view. Further evidence is adduced in Chapter 11, where various aspects of children's use of modal expressions appear to be in line with what one might have predicted on the basis of the analysis in Chapters 3 to 9, together with what is known about cognitive development.

As well as being able to provide a guide to an area of language which has been relatively little discussed elsewhere, the analysis proposed above has afforded a new perspective on the modals (Chapter 3) which have been widely discussed by linguists, and, in addition, has made it possible to view in a new light such key areas of language as tense, IF-clauses, and questions, which may also be regarded as expressing modality.

Besides discussing a range of specific issues that relate to modality, I have tried to show generally that although form is an obvious and necessary focus for linguistics, it can never, by itself, provide anything like a complete picture of language, and in fact may not even be the best starting point in some cases. Although the scope of this book is broad, it is because of its breadth that it has been possible to show how many different considerations are brought to bear on linguistic form. Syntax is merely a nexus—a meeting point of semantics and pragmatics, and although it is amenable to formalization as an autonomous phenomenon, it should not be forgotten that the notion of autonomous syntax is a theoretical abstraction. In the case of modality, it is only when the different perspectives of philosophy and philosophical logic (Chapter 2), semantics and syntax (Chapters 3 to 9), pragmatics and social interaction (Chapter 10), child language acquisition and developmental psychology (Chapter 11) are all brought into focus at the same time that one begins to feel that one has grasped something like an understanding of what modality actually is.

Clearly, a book of this length cannot do much more than focus the mind on a number of related issues. It can certainly not do justice to each individual perspective of modality; but clarifying what similarities do exist makes it possible to take a new look at each independent discipline, and in some cases to envisage one or two new areas which might fruitfully be explored.

In the case of linguistics, Brown and Levinson's (1978: 147) conclusion that 'indirect speech acts have as their prime *raison d'être* the politeness functions they perform' and that 'their internal structure is best accounted for as conforming with the demands of particular politeness strategies' used according to rational principles, is highly relevant to the present study, since the linguistic device which figures most prominently in indirect speech acts is the modal expression. Brown and Levinson further note that it seems highly likely that 'indirect speech acts are universal and for the most part are probably constructed in essentially similar ways in all languages'. If this is, in fact, the case, the analysis of modal expressions in this book which shows them to be a semantically, as well as a pragmatically, coherent class, should prove to be broadly applicable to similar expressions in other languages. If further research reveals similar scales of formal explicitness and subjectivity/objectivity within the same semantic framework, the validity of the system of analysis used here will be further enhanced.

There is also much here which is highly relevant to future research into child language acquisition. Studies of modal expressions in child language have to date been based largely on syntactic descriptions of the adult language and have thus been mainly restricted to modal auxiliary verbs. The few studies of categories like tense and IF-clauses, often related to cognitive development, are not seen to be related in any obvious linguistic sense. However, the findings reported in Chapter 11 suggest that our understanding of the various ways of expressing modality in English could be greatly improved if future research were carried out within some such overall framework as that suggested here. The relevance of modality to moral judgement suggests that studies of linguistic development might well benefit from an awareness of the views of Piaget (1932) and the numerous publications of Kohlberg (cf. Tomlinson, 1980). Also, the period of linguistic development from 5 up to adolescence is an area which is particularly ripe for research, in view of the virtual absence of certain categories of modal expression observed in the spontaneous speech of children as old as 12.

Throughout the book I have tried not to lose sight of the concept of modality itself. The various dimensions of modality which have been explored may be ultimately traced back to the effect of a single fundamental human trait on language and thought. This trait, which was described in 2.1 in terms of a basic worldview according to which it is possible to conceive of things being otherwise, is the motivating force behind what has been variously described here in terms of syntax, semantics, pragmatics, and developmental psychology. Although the nature of this enigmatic core of modality still remains something of a mystery, it is hoped that what has been said here will have gone some way towards accounting for the way in which modality is manifested in the more tangible medium of language, and that the areas that have been mapped will consequently appear a little less mysterious.

Bibliography

Ackrill, J. L. (1963), *Aristotle's Categories and De Interpretatione Translated with Notes and a Glossary*, Oxford, Oxford University Press.

Aitken, A., McIntosh, A. and Palsson, H. (eds) (1971), *Edinburgh Studies in English and Scots*, London, Longman.

Akmajian, A. and Heny, F. W. (1975), *An Introduction to the Principles of Transformational Syntax*, Cambridge, Mass., MIT Press.

Alexandrescu, S. (1976), 'Sur les modalités *croire et savoir*', *Langages* 43, 19–27.

Allerton, D. J., Carney, E. and Holdcroft, D. (eds) (1979), *Function and Context in Linguistic Analysis: A Festschrift for William Haas*, Cambridge, Cambridge University Press.

Anderson, J. (1971), 'Some proposals concerning the modal verb in English' in Aitken *et al.* (1971: 69–120).

Anderson, J. M. and Jones, C. (eds) (1974), *Historical Linguistics I: Proceedings of the First International Conference on Historical Linguistics*, Amsterdam, North Holland.

Antinucci, F. and Miller, R. (1976), 'How children talk about what happened', *Journal of Child Language* 3, 167–89.

Antinucci, F. and Parisi, D. (1971), 'On English modal verbs' in *Papers from the Seventh Regional Meeting of the Chicago Linguistic Society*, Chicago, Department of Linguistics, University of Chicago, pp. 28–39.

Antinucci, F. and Parisi, D. (1973), 'Early language acquisition: A model and some data' in Ferguson and Slobin (1973: 607–19).

Aristotle, *De Interpretatione*.

Austin, J. L. (1962), *How to Do Things With Words*, Oxford, Clarendon Press.

Bates, E. (1976), *Language and Context: The Acquisition of Pragmatics*, New York, Academic Press.

Bazell, C. E., Catford, J. C., Halliday, M. A. K. and Robins, R. H. (eds) (1966), *In Memory of J. R. Firth*, London, Longman.

Bellert, I. (1977), 'On semantic and distributional properties of sentential adverbs', *Linguistic Inquiry* 8, 337–51.

Bernstein, B. (1962), 'Social class, linguistic codes and grammatical elements', *Language and Speech* 5, 31–46.

Bernstein, B. (ed) (1973), *Class, Codes and Control, Vol. 2: Applied Studies Towards a Sociology of Language*, London, Routledge and Kegan Paul.

Bierwisch, M. and Heidolph, K. (eds) (1970), *Progress in Linguistics*, The Hague, Mouton.

Binnick, R. I. (1971), '*Will* and *Be Going To*' in *Papers from the Seventh Regional Meeting of the Chicago Linguistic Society*, Chicago, Department of Linguistics, University of Chicago, pp. 40–52.

Binnick, R. I. (1972), '*Will* and *Be Going To* II' in *Papers from the Eighth*

Regional Meeting of the Chicago Linguistic Society, Chicago, Department of Linguistics, University of Chicago, pp. 3–9.

Bloom, L. (1970), *Language Development: Form and Function in Emerging Grammars*, Cambridge, Mass., MIT Press.

Bloom, L. (1973), *One Word at a Time*, The Hague, Mouton.

Boden, M. A. (1979), *Piaget*, Glasgow, Fontana.

Bolinger, D. (1977), *Meaning and Form*, London, Longman.

Bouma, L. (1975), 'On contrasting the semantics of the modal auxiliaries of German and English', *Lingua* 37, 313–39.

Boyd, J. and Thorne, J. P. (1969), 'The deep grammar of modal verbs', *Journal of Linguistics* 5, 57–74.

Bresnan, J. (1978), 'A realistic transformational grammar' in Halle *et al.* (1978: 1–59).

Brown, P. and Levinson, S. (1978), 'Universals in language usage: Politeness phenomena' in Goody (1978a: 56–289).

Brown, R. (1970), *Psycholinguistics*, New York, The Free Press.

Brown, R. (1973), *A First Language: The Early Stages*, London, Allen and Unwin.

Brown, R., Cazden, C. and Bellugi, U. (1969), 'The child's grammar from I to III' in Hill (1969).

Brown, R. and Hanlon, C. (1970), 'Derivational complexity and the order of acquisition in child speech', in Hayes (1970: 11–53).

Bruner, J. S. (1978), 'Learning how to do things with words' in Bruner and Garton (1978: 62–84).

Bruner, J. S. and Garton, A. (eds) (1978), *Human Growth and Development*, Oxford, Clarendon Press.

Butler, C. S. (1972), 'A contrastive study of modality in English, French, German and Italian', *Nottingham Linguistic Circular* 2, 26–39.

Calbert, J. (1975), 'Towards the semantics of modality', in Calbert and Vater (1975: 1–70).

Calbert, J. and Vater, H. (eds) (1975), *Aspekte der Modalität (Studien zur Deutschen Grammatik, I)*, Tübingen, Verlag Gunter Narr.

Cambon, J. and Sinclair, H. (1974), 'Relations between syntax and semantics: Are they "easy to see"?', *British Journal of Psychology* 65, 133–40.

Cheng, R. L. (1980), 'Modality in Taiwanese', *Journal of the Chinese Language Teachers Association* 15, 45–93.

Chomsky, C. (1969), *The Acquisition of Syntax in Children from 5 to 10*, Cambridge, Mass., MIT Press.

Classification of Occupations 1970, London, Her Majesty's Stationery Office.

Close, R. A. (1962), *English as a Foreign Language*, London, Longman.

Coates, J. (1980), 'On the non-equivalence of *may* and *can*', *Lingua* 50, 209–20.

Coates, J. (1983), *The Semantics of the Modal Auxiliaries*, London, Croom Helm.

Cole, P. and Morgan, J. L. (eds) (1975), *Syntax and Semantics, 3: Speech Acts*, New York, Academic Press.

Coleman, J. C. (ed) (1979), *The School Years: Current Issues in the Socialization of Young People*, London: Methuen.

Collins, P. (1974), 'The analysis of the English "modal auxiliaries" as main verbs', *Kivung* 7, 151–66.

Corum, C. (1975), 'A pragmatic analysis of parenthetic adjuncts' in *Papers from the Eleventh Regional Meeting of the Chicago Linguistic*

Society, Chicago, Department of Linguistics, University of Chicago, pp. 131–41.

Cromer, R. (1970), 'Children are nice to understand: Surface structure clues for the recovery of deep structure', *British Journal of Psychology* 61, 397–408.

Cromer, R. (1971), 'The development of the ability to decenter in time', *British Journal of Psychology* 62, 353–65.

Crystal, D. (1966), 'Specification and English tenses', *Journal of Linguistics* 2, 1–34.

Crystal, D. (1969), *Prosodic Systems and Intonation in English*, Cambridge, Cambridge University Press.

Crystal, D. (1975), *The English Tone of Voice*, London, Arnold.

Darden, B. J. (1973), 'On confirmative tag sentences in English' in *Papers from the Ninth Regional Meeting of the Chicago Linguistic Society*, Chicago, Department of Linguistics, University of Chicago, pp. 104–13.

Davies, E. C. (1979), *On the Semantics of Syntax*, London, Croom Helm.

Donaldson, M. (1978), *Children's Minds*, Glasgow, Fontana.

Downes, W. (1977), 'The imperative and pragmatics', *Journal of Linguistics* 13, 17–97.

Ehrman, M. (1966), *The Meanings of the Modals in Present Day English*, The Hague, Mouton.

Emerson, H. F. (1980), 'Children's judgements of correct and reversed sentences with "if" ', *Journal of Child Language* 7, 137–55.

Emmerich, P. J. (1969), 'The Psychological Correlates of the English Modal Auxiliary System', Ph.D. Thesis, University of Nebraska.

Ervin, S. (1964), 'Imitation and structural change in children's language' in Lenneberg (1964).

Fawcett, R. P. (1980), *Cognitive Linguistics and Social Interaction: Towards an Integrated Model of a Systemic Functional Grammar and the Other Components of a Communicating Mind*, Heidelberg, Julius Groos.

Fawcett, R. P. and Perkins, M. R. (1980), *Child Language Transcripts 6–12, 4 Vols.*, Pontypridd, Department of Behavioural and Communication Studies, Polytechnic of Wales.

Fawcett, R. P. and Perkins, M. R. (1981), 'Project report: Language development in 6 to 12 year old children', *First Language* 2, 75–9.

Ferguson, C. A. and Slobin, D. I. (eds) (1973), *Studies of Child Language Development*, New York, Holt, Rinehart and Winston.

Ferreiro, E. and Sinclair, H. (1971), 'Temporal relationships in language', *International Journal of Psychology* 6, 39–47.

Fielding, G. and Fraser, C. (1978), 'Language and interpersonal relations' in Markova (1978: 217–32).

Fitikides, T. J. (1963), *Common Mistakes in English (5th ed.)*, London, Longman.

Fletcher, P. (1975), Review of Major (1974), *Journal of Child Language* 2, 318–22.

Fletcher, P. (1979), 'The development of the verb phrase' in Fletcher and Garman (1979: 261–84).

Fletcher, P. and Garman, M. (eds) (1979), *Language Acquisition*, Cambridge, Cambridge University Press.

Fodor, J. D. (1977), *Semantics: Theories of Meaning in Generative Grammar*, New York, T. Y. Crowell.

Fraser, B. (1975), 'Hedged performatives' in Cole and Morgan (1975: 187–210).

Fraser, C. and Scherer, K. R. (eds) (1982), *Advances in the Social Psychology of Language*, Cambridge, Cambridge University Press and Paris, Edition de la Maison des Sciences de l'Homme.

Fries, C. C. (1927), 'The expression of the future', *Language* 3, 87–95.

Fujimura, O. (ed) (1973), *Three Dimensions of Linguistic Theory*, Tokyo, The TEC Company.

Geis, M. L. (1979), Review of Bolinger (1977), *Language* 55, 684–7.

Gibbs, R. W. Jr. (1981), 'Your wish is my command: Convention and context in interpreting indirect requests', *Journal of Verbal Learning and Verbal Behaviour* 20, 431–44.

Goody, E. N. (ed) (1978a), *Questions and Politeness: Strategies in Social Interaction*, Cambridge, Cambridge University Press.

Goody, E. N. (1978b), 'Towards a theory of questions' in Goody (1978a: 17–43).

Gordon, D. and Lakoff, G. (1971), 'Conversational postulates' in *Papers from the Seventh Regional Meeting of the Chicago Linguistic Society*, Chicago, Department of Linguistics, University of Chicago, pp. 63–84.

Green, G. M. (1975), 'How to get people to do things with words: The whimperative question' in Cole and Morgan (1975: 107–41).

Greenbaum, S. (1969), *Studies in English Adverbial Usage*, London, Longman.

Greenbaum, S. (1974), 'Problems in the negation of modals', *Moderna Språk* 68, 244–66.

Grice, H. P. (1968), 'Utterer's meaning, sentence-meaning, and word-meaning', *Foundations of Language* 4, 1–18.

Griffiths, P. (1979), 'Speech acts and early sentences' in Fletcher and Garman (1979: 105–20).

Gruber, J. S. (1973), 'Correlation between the syntactic constructions of the child and of the adult' in Ferguson and Slobin (1973: 440–5).

Haack, S. (1978), *Philosophy of Logics*, Cambridge, Cambridge University Press.

Hacking, I. (1967), 'Possibility', *Philosophical Review* 76, 143–68.

Haegeman, L. (1980), '*Have to* and progressive aspect', *Journal of English Linguistics* 14, 1–5.

Haegeman. L. (1981), 'Modal *shall* and speaker's control', *Journal of English Linguistics* 15, 4–9.

Halle, M., Bresnan, J. and Miller, G. A. (eds) (1978), *Linguistic Theory and Psychological Reality*, Cambridge, Mass., MIT Press.

Halliday, M. A. K. (1970a), 'Functional diversity in language, as seen from a consideration of modality and mood in English', *Foundations of Language* 6, 322–61.

Halliday, M. A. K. (1970b), 'Language structure and language function' in Lyons (1970: 140–65).

Halliday, M. A. K. (1970c), *A Course in Spoken English: Intonation*, Oxford, Oxford University Press.

Halliday, M. A. K. (1973), *Explorations in the Functions of Language*, London, Arnold.

Halliday, M. A. K. (1975), *Learning How to Mean: Explorations in the Development of Language*, London, Arnold.

Halpern, R. N. (1975), 'Time travel or the futuristic use of "to go" ', *Studies in The Linguistic Sciences* 5, 36–41.

Hancher, M. (1979), 'The classification of cooperative illocutionary acts', *Language in Society* 8, 1–14.

Harre, R. (1959), 'Modal expressions in ordinary and technical language', *Australasian Journal of Philosophy* 37, 41–56.

Hartmann, R. R. K. (ed) (1977), *Papers in German–English Contrastive Applied Linguistics*, Coleraine, The New University of Ulster.

Hayes, J. R. (ed) (1970), *Cognition and the Development of Language*, New York, John Wiley.

Hedenius, I. (1963), 'Performatives', *Theoria* 29, 115–36.

Henderson, B. L. K. (1945), *The English Way: A Text-book on the Art of Writing (2nd ed.)*, London, Macdonald and Evans.

Hermerén, L. (1978), *On Modality in English: A Study of the Semantics of the Modals (Lund Studies in English, 53)*, Lund, C. W. K. Gleerup.

Hill, J. (ed) (1969), *Minnesota Symposia on Child Psychology, Vol. II*, Minneapolis, University of Minneapolis Press.

Hintikka, J. (1962), *Knowledge and Belief: An Introduction to the Logic of the Two Notions*, Ithaca, Cornell University Press.

Hintikka, J. (1979), ' "Is", semantical games, and semantical relativity', *Journal of Philosophical Logic* 8, 443–68.

Hirst, W. and Weil, J. (1982), 'Acquisition of epistemic and deontic meaning of modals', *Journal of Child Language* 9, 659–66.

Hofmann, T. R. (1966), 'Past tense replacement and the modal system', in *Harvard Computational Laboratory Report to the National Science Foundation on Mathematical Linguistics and Automatic Translation, No. NSF-17*, Cambridge, Mass.

Holmberg, A. (1979), 'On whimperatives and related questions', *Journal of Linguistics* 15, 225–44.

Householder, F. W. (1971), *Linguistic Speculations*, London, Cambridge University Press.

Huddleston, R. D. (1971), *The Sentence in Written English: A Syntactic Study Based on an Analysis of Scientific Texts*, Cambridge, Cambridge University Press.

Huddleston, R. D. (1978), 'On the constituent structure of VP and Aux', *Linguistic Analysis* 4, 31–59.

Huddleston, R. D. (1979), '*Would have become*: empty or modal WILL?', *Journal of Linguistics* 15, 335–40.

Hudson, R. A. (1975), 'The meaning of questions', *Language* 51, 1–31.

Hughes, A. and Trudgill, P. (1979), *English Accents and Dialects: An Introduction to Social and Regional Varieties of British English*, London, Arnold.

Hunt, K. W. (1964), *Differences in Grammatical Structures Written at Three Grade Levels, the Structures to be Analyzed by Transformations*, Report to U.S. Office of Education, Cooperative Research Project No. 1998, Tallahassee, Florida.

Hunt, K. W. (1965), *Grammatical Structures Written at Three Grade Levels*, Champaign, Ill., National Council of Teachers of English, Research Report No. 3.

Hunt, K. W. (1970), *Syntactic Maturity in Children and Adults, Monographs of the Society for Research in Child Development No. 134*.

Ingram, D. (1975), 'If and when transformations are acquired by children', *Georgetown University Round Table on Languages and Linguistics 1975*, pp. 99–127.

Jackendoff, R. (1972), *Semantic Interpretation in Generative Grammar*, Cambridge, Mass., MIT Press.

Jacobs, R. A. and Rosenbaum, P. S. (eds) (1970), *Readings in English Transformational Grammar*, Waltham, Mass., Ginn.

Jarvella, R. J. and Klein, W. (eds) (1982), *Speech, Place, and Action: Studies in Deixis and Related Topics*, Chichester, Wiley.

Jenkins, L. (1972), '*Will*-deletion' in *Papers from the Eighth Regional Meeting of the Chicago Linguistic Society*, Chicago, Department of Linguistics, University of Chicago, pp. 173–82.

Jespersen, O. (1924), *The Philosophy of Grammar*, London, George Allen and Unwin.

Jespersen, O. (1931), *A Modern English Grammar, Vol. IV*, London, George Allen and Unwin.

Joos, M. (1964), *The English Verb*, Madison and Milwaukee, University of Wisconsin Press.

Kaper, W. (1980), 'The use of the past tense in games of pretend', *Journal of Child Language* 7, 213–15.

Karmiloff-Smith, A. (1979), 'Language development after five' in Fletcher and Garman (1979: 307–23).

Karttunen, L. (1971), 'Some observations on factivity', *Papers in Linguistics* 4, 55–69.

Karttunen, L. (1972), '*Possible* and *must*' in Kimball (1972: 1–20).

Katz, J. J. (1977), *Propositional Structure and Illocutionary Force: A Study of the Contribution of Sentence Meaning to Speech Acts*, Sussex, Harvester Press.

Keenan, E. O., Schiefflin, B. B. and Platt, M. (1978), 'Questions of immediate concern' in Goody (1978a: 44–55).

Kemp, J. A. (1972), *John Wallis's Grammar of the English Language*, London, Longman.

Kempson, R. M. (1977), *Semantic Theory*, Cambridge, Cambridge University Press.

Kenny, A. (1975), *Will, Freedom and Power*, Oxford, Basil Blackwell.

Kimball, J. P. (ed) (1972), *Syntax and Semantics, Vol. I*, New York, Academic Press.

Kiparsky, P. and Kiparsky, C. (1970), 'Fact' in Bierwisch and Heidolph (1970: 143–73).

Klann-Delius, G. (1981), 'Sex and language acquisition—is there any influence?', *Journal of Pragmatics* 5, 1–25.

Klima, E. S. and Bellugi, U. (1966), 'Syntactic peculiarities in the speech of children' in Lyons and Wales (1966: 183–208).

Kratzer, A. (1977), 'What "must" and "can" must and can mean', *Linguistics and Philosophy* 1, 337–55.

Kress, G. (1977), 'Tense as a modality', *University of East Anglia Papers in Linguistics*, pp. 40–52.

Kruisinga, E. (1932), *A Handbook of Present-Day English: Part II: English Accidence and Syntax Vol. 3 (5th ed.)*, Groningen, P. Noordhoff.

Kuczaj, S. A. (1977), 'Old and new forms, old and new meanings: the form-function hypothesis revisited', Paper presented at the meeting of the Society for Research on Child Development, New Orleans.

Kuczaj, S. A. and Daly, M. J. (1979), 'The development of hypothetical reference in the speech of young children', *Journal of Child Language* 6, 563–79.

Kuczaj, S. and Maratsos, M. (1975), 'What a child CAN say before he WILL', *Merrill-Palmer Quarterly* 21, 89–111.

Lakoff, R. (1969), 'A syntactic argument for negative transportation', in *Papers from the Fifth Regional Meeting of the Chicago Linguistic Society*, Chicago, Department of Linguistics, University of Chicago, pp. 140–7.

Lakoff, R. (1972a), 'The pragmatics of modality', in *Papers from the Eighth Regional Meeting of the Chicago Linguistic Society*, Chicago, Department of Linguistics, University of Chicago, pp. 229–46.

Lakoff, R. (1972b), 'Language in context', *Language* 48, 907–27.

Lakoff, R. (1975), *Language and Woman's Place*, New York, Harper and Row.

Larkin, D. (1976), 'Some notes on English modals' in McCawley (1976: 387–98).

Lee, D. A. (1975), 'Modal "auxiliaries" in generative grammar—some pedagogical implications', *International Review of Applied Linguistics* 13, 263–74.

Lee, V. (ed) (1979), *Language Development*, London, Open University Press.

Leech, G. N. (1969), *Towards a Semantic Description of English*, London, Longman.

Leech, G. N. (1971), *Meaning and the English Verb*, London, Longman.

Leech, G. N. (1977), Review of Sadock (1974) and Cole and Morgan (1975), *Journal of Linguistics* 13, 133–45.

Leech, G. N. and Svartvik, J. (1975), *A Communicative Grammar of English*, London, Longman.

Lemmon, E. J. (1962), 'On sentences verifiable by their use', *Analysis* 22, 86–9.

Lenneberg, E. (ed) (1964), *New Directions in the Study of Language*, Cambridge, Mass., MIT Press.

Leopold, W. (1949), *Speech Development of a Bilingual Child, Vol. IV, Diary from Age 2*, Evanston, Ill., Northwestern University Press.

Levinson, S. C. (1980), 'Speech act theory: the state of the art', *Language Teaching and Linguistics Abstracts* 13, 5–24.

Lightfoot, D. (1974), 'The diachronic analysis of English modals' in Anderson and Jones (1974: 219–49).

Loban, W. D. (1961), *The Language of Elementary School Children*, Champaign, Ill., National Council of Teachers of English.

Loban, W. D. (1966), *Language Ability: Grades Seven, Eight and Nine*, Washington, Cooperative Research Monograph No. 18, U.S. Department of Health, Education and Welfare, Office of Education.

Lodge, K. R. (1974), 'Modality and Modal Verbs in English and German', Ph.D. Thesis, University of East Anglia.

Lodge, K. R. (1977), 'The modal verbs' in Hartmann (1977: 46–54).

Lodge, K. R. (1979), 'The use of the past tense in games of pretend', *Journal of Child Language* 6, 365–9.

Long, R. B. (1961), *The Sentence and its Parts*, Chicago, University of Chicago Press.

Lucas, J. R. (1973), *A Treatise on Time and Space*, London, Methuen.

Lyons, J. (1968), *Introduction to Theoretical Linguistics*, Cambridge, Cambridge University Press.

Lyons, J. (ed) (1970), *New Horizons in Linguistics*, Harmondsworth, Penguin.

Lyons, J. (1977), *Semantics*, London, Cambridge University Press.

Lyons, J. (1982), 'Deixis and subjectivity: *loquor, ergo sum?*' in Jarvella and Klein (1982: 101–24).

Lyons, J. and Wales, R. J. (eds) (1966), *Psycholinguistic Papers*, Edinburgh, Edinburgh University Press.

McCawley, J. D. (ed) (1976), *Syntax and Semantics, Vol. 7: Notes from the Linguistic Underground*, New York, Academic Press.

McCawley, J. D. (1981), *Everything that Linguists Have Always Wanted to Know about Logic (but Were Ashamed to Ask)*, Oxford, Blackwell.

McIntosh, A. (1966), 'Predictive statements' in Bazell *et al.* (1966: 303-20).

Major, D. (1974), *The Acquisition of Modal Auxiliaries in the Language of Children*, The Hague, Mouton.

Marino, M. (1973), 'A feature analysis of the modal system of English', *Lingua* 32, 309-23.

Markova, I. (ed) (1978), *The Social Context of Language*, Chichester, Wiley.

Menyuk, P. (1969), *Sentences Children Use*, Cambridge, Mass., MIT Press.

Miller, G. A. (1978), 'Semantic relations among words' in Halle *et al.* (1978: 60-118).

Miller, G. A. and Johnson-Laird, P. N. (1976), *Language and Perception*, Cambridge, Cambridge University Press.

Miller, W. R. (1973), 'The acquisition of grammatical rules in English' in Ferguson and Slobin (1973: 380-91).

Modgil, S. and Modgil, C. (eds) (1980), *Toward a Theory of Psychological Development*, Windsor, Berks., N.F.E.R. Publishing Co.

Mohan, B. A. (1974), 'Principles, postulates, politeness' in *Papers from the Tenth Regional Meeting of the Chicago Linguistic Society*, Chicago, Department of Linguistics, University of Chicago, pp. 446-59.

Moore, T. E. (ed) (1973), *Cognitive Development and the Acquisition of Language*, New York, Academic Press.

Mussen, P. H. (ed) (1970), *Carmichael's Handbook of Child Psychology*, New York, John Wiley.

Newmeyer, F. J. (1975), *English Aspectual Verbs*, The Hague, Mouton.

Ney, J. W. (1976), 'The modals in English: A floating semantic feature analysis', *Journal of English Linguistics* 10, 8-20.

O'Donnell, R., Griffin, W. and Norris, W. (1967), *Syntax of Kindergarten and Elementary School Children: A Transformational Analysis*, Champaign-Urbana, Ill., National Council of Teachers of English.

O'Donnell, W. R. (1977), Review of Palmer (1974), *Journal of Linguistics* 13, 128-33.

Opdycke, J. B. (1946), *Don't Say It: A Cyclopedia of English Use and Abuse (4th ed.)*, New York, Funk and Wagnalls.

Palmer, F. R. (1974), *The English Verb*, London, Longman.

Palmer, F. R. (1977), 'Modals and actuality', *Journal of Linguistics* 13, 1-23.

Palmer, F. R. (1978), 'Past tense transportation: a reply', *Journal of Linguistics* 14, 77-81.

Palmer, F. R. (1979a), *Modality and the English Modals*, London, Longman.

Palmer, F. R. (1979b), 'Why auxiliaries are not main verbs', *Lingua* 47, 1-25.

Palmer, F. R. (1979c), 'Non-assertion and modality' in Allerton *et al.* (1979: 185-95).

Perkins, M. R. (1980), 'The Expression of Modality in English', Ph.D. Thesis, The Polytechnic of Wales, C.N.A.A.

Perkins, M. R. (1981), 'The development of modal expressions in the spontaneous speech of 6- to 12-year-old children', *Work in Progress* (Edinburgh University) 14, 54-61.

Perkins, M. R. (1982), 'The core meanings of the English modals', *Journal of Linguistics* 18, 245-73.

Phythian, B. A. (1980), *English Grammar*, Bungay, Hodder and Stoughton.

Piaget, J. (1926), *Judgement and Reasoning in the Child*, London, Routledge and Kegan Paul.

Piaget, J. (1932), *The Moral Judgement of the Child*, London, Routledge and Kegan Paul.

Piaget, J. (1970), 'Piaget's theory' in Mussen (1970: 703–32).

Piaget, J. and Inhelder, B. (1958), *The Growth of Logical Thinking: From Childhood to Adolescence*, London, Routledge and Kegan Paul.

Pottier, B. (1976), 'Sur la formulation des modalités en linguistique', *Langages*, 43, 39–46.

Poutsma, H. (1924), *A Grammar of Late Modern English, Part I*, Groningen, Noordhoff.

Prior, A. N. (1957), *Time and Modality*, Oxford, Oxford University Press.

Pullum, G. and Wilson, D. (1977), 'Autonomous syntax and the analysis of auxiliaries', *Language* 53, 741–88.

Quirk, R., Greenbaum, S., Leech, G. and Svartvik, J. (1972), *A Grammar of Contemporary English*, London, Longman.

Ramge, H. (1973), *Spracherweb: Grundzuge der Sprachentwicklung des Kindes*, Tübingen, Niemeyer.

Ransom, E. (1977), 'On the representation of modality', *Linguistics and Philosophy* 1, 357–79.

Reichenbach, H. (1947), *Elements of Symbolic Logic*, New York, Free Press.

Rescher, N. (1968), *Topics in Philosophical Logic*, Dordrecht, Reidel.

Rescher, N. (1979), *Leibniz: An Introduction to his Philosophy*, Oxford, Blackwell.

Richardson, K., Calnan, M., Essen, J. and Lambert, L. (1976), 'The linguistic maturity of 11-year-olds: Some analysis of the written composition of children in the National Child Development Study', *Journal of Child Language* 3, 99–115.

Rosenbaum, P. S. (1967), *The Grammar of English Predicate Complement Constructions*, Cambridge, Mass., MIT Press.

Rosenberg, M. S. (1975), 'Factives that aren't so' in *Papers from the Eleventh Regional Meeting of the Chicago Linguistic Society*, Chicago, Department of Linguistics, University of Chicago, pp. 475–86.

Ross, J. R. (1970), 'On declarative sentences' in Jacobs and Rosenbaum (1970: 222–72).

Ross, J. R. (1972), 'The category squish: endstation Hauptwort' in *Papers from the Eighth Regional Meeting of the Chicago Linguistic Society*, Chicago, Department of Linguistics, University of Chicago, pp. 316–28.

Ross, J. R. (1973), 'Nouniness' in Fujimura (1973: 137–257).

Rudin, C. (1977), 'Toward a unified treatment of *will*', *Language Sciences* 48, 14–16.

Ryle, G. (1949), *The Concept of Mind*, London, Hutchinson.

Sadock, J. (1970), 'Whimperatives' in Sadock and Vanek (1970: 223–38).

Sadock, J. M. (1974), *Toward a Linguistic Theory of Speech Acts*, New York, Academic Press.

Sadock, J. and Vanek, A. (eds) (1970), *Studies Presented to Robert B. Lees by his Students*, Edmonton, Ill., Linguistic Research Inc.

Savić, S. (1975), 'Aspects of adult–child communication: The problem of question acquisition', *Journal of Child Language* 2, 251–60.

Scheurweghs, G. (1959), *Present-Day English Syntax: A Survey of Sentence Patterns*, London, Longman.

Schwartz, S. P. (1977), *Naming, Necessity and Natural Kinds*, Ithaca, Cornell University Press.

Scott, C. M. (1982), Review of Fawcett and Perkins (1980), *Journal of Child Language* 9, 704–8.

Searle, J. R. (1975), 'Indirect speech acts' in Cole and Morgan (1975: 59–82).

Searle, J. R. (1976), 'The classification of illocutionary acts', *Language in Society* 5, 1–23.

Searle, J. R. (1979), *Expression and Meaning*, Cambridge, Cambridge University Press.

Seiler, H. (1971), 'Abstract structures for moods in Greek', *Language* 47, 79–89.

Seuren, P. A. M. (1969), *Operators and Nucleus*, Cambridge, Cambridge University Press.

Sheintuch, G. and Wise, K. (1976), 'On the pragmatic unity of the rules of Neg-Raising and Neg-Attraction' in *Papers from the Twelfth Regional Meeting of the Chicago Linguistic Society*, Chicago, Department of Linguistics, University of Chicago, pp. 548–57.

Shields, M. M. (1974), 'The development of the modal auxiliary system', *Birmingham Educational Review* 26, 180–200.

Shorter Oxford English Dictionary on Historical Principles (Reset with Revised Etymologies and Addenda), Oxford, Oxford University Press.

Shou-Hsin, T. (1980), 'The semantics and syntax of modal verbs in Amoy', *Journal of the Chinese Language Teachers Association* 15, 33–44.

Simone, R. and Amacker, R. (1977), 'Verbi "modali" in italiano', *Italian Linguistics* 3, 7–102.

Sinclair-de Zwart, H. (1973), 'Language acquisition and cognitive development' in Moore (1973: 9–25).

Slobin, D. I. (ed) (1971), *The Ontogenesis of Grammar*, New York, Academic Press.

Slobin, D. I. (1973), 'Cognitive prerequisites for the development of grammar' in Ferguson and Slobin (1973: 175–208).

Smith, C. (1980), 'The acquisition of time talk: Relations between child and adult grammars', *Journal of Child Language* 7, 263–78.

Smith, N. and Wilson, D. (1979), *Modern Linguistics: The Results of Chomsky's Revolution*, Harmondsworth, Penguin.

Sohn, H. M. (1974), 'Modals and speaker–hearer perspectives in Korean', *Papers in Linguistics* 7, 493–520.

Stampe, D. W. (1975), 'Meaning and truth in the theory of speech acts' in Cole and Morgan (1975: 1–39).

Standwell, G. J. B. (1979), 'A contrastive study of the modals in English and German', *International Review of Applied Linguistics* 17, 251–64.

Steele, S. (1975), 'Is it possible?', *Stanford University Working Papers on Language Universals* 18, 35–58.

Stockwell, R. P., Schachter, P. and Partee, B. H. (1973), *The Major Syntactic Structures of English*, New York, Holt, Rinehart and Winston.

Strang, B. M. H. (1970), *A History of English*, London, Methuen.

Stratton, C. (1940), *Handbook of English*, New York, Whittlesey House.

Sweet, H. (1898), *A New English Grammar, Logical and Historical*, Oxford, Oxford University Press.

Tomlinson, P. (1980), 'Moral judgement and moral psychology: Piaget, Kohlberg and beyond' in Modgil and Modgil (1980: 303–66).

Traugott, E. C. (1972), *The History of English Syntax: A Transformational Approach to the History of English Sentence Structure*, New York, Holt, Rinehart and Winston.

Treble, H. A. and Vallins, G. H. (1936), *An A.B.C. of English Usage*, Oxford, Oxford University Press.

Trudgill, P. and Hannah, J. (1982), *International English: A Guide to Varieties of Standard English*, London, Arnold.

Turner, G. J. (1973), 'Social class and children's language of control at age five and age seven' in Bernstein (1973: 135–201).

Turner, G. and Pickvance, R. (1972), 'Social class differences in the expression of uncertainty in five year old children's speech and language', *Language and Speech* 14, 303–25.

Turner, J. (1975), *Cognitive Development*, London, Methuen.

Ultan, R. (1972), 'The nature of future tenses', *Working Papers on Language Universals* 8, 55–100.

Urmson, J. O. (1952), 'Parenthetical verbs', *Mind* 61, 480–96.

Von Wright, G. H. (1951), *An Essay in Modal Logic*, Amsterdam, North Holland.

Waterson, N. and Snow, C. (eds) (1978), *The Development of Communication*, Chichester, John Wiley.

Weinreich-Haste, H. (1979), 'Moral development' in Coleman (1979: 46–78).

Wekker, H. Chr. (1976), *The Expression of Future Time in Contemporary British English*, Amsterdam, North Holland.

Wells, C. G. (1979), 'Learning and using the auxiliary verb in English' in Lee (1979: 250–70).

Wells, C. G. (1981), *Learning Through Interaction: The Study of Language Development (Language at Home and at School, Vol. I)*, Cambridge, Cambridge University Press.

Wells, C. G. and Robinson, W. P. (1982), 'The role of adult speech in language development' in Fraser and Scherer (1982: 11–76).

Wells, J. C. (1982), *Accents of English, Vol. 2: The British Isles*, Cambridge, Cambridge University Press.

Wertheimer, R. (1972), *The Significance of Sense: Meaning, Modality and Morality*, Ithaca, Cornell University Press.

West, M. and Kimber, P. F. (1957), *Deskbook of Correct English*, London, Longmans, Green and Co.

White, A. (1975), *Modal Thinking*, Oxford, Blackwell.

Young, D. J. (1980), *The Structure of English Clauses*, London, Hutchinson.

Zandvoort, R. W. (1975), *A Handbook of English Grammar (7th ed.)*, London, Longman.

Name Index

Modal Expressions Index *

ABILITY, 87
ABLE TO, 53, 68, 74-6, 88n., 122, 131, 141, 148, 151
ABOUT TO, 72-3
ADVERTISED, 82-3
ADVISE, 95
ADVISED, 83
ADVOCATE, 95
ADVOCATED, 83
AFFIRM, 94
AFFIRMATION, 86
AFFIRMED, 82-3
ALLEGATION, 86
ALLEGE, 94
ALLEGED, 82-3
ALLEGEDLY, 89
ALLOW, 95, 102
ALLOWED, 84-5, 141, 145
APPARENT, 81, 93
APPARENTLY, 89
APPEAR, 79, 98, 123
APT TO, 70, 74
ARGUABLE, 85
ARGUABLY, 89
ARGUE, 94
ARGUED, 82-3
ARGUMENT, 86
ASK, 95
ASKED, 83
ASSERT, 94-7, 156
ASSERTED, 82-3
ASSERTION, 86
ASSUME, 97
ASSUMED, 83-4
ASSUMPTION, 86
ATTEST, 94
ATTESTED, 82-3
AUTHORIZATION, 102
AUTHORIZE, 95, 102-3
AUTHORIZED, 83
AVER, 94
AVERRED, 82-3

BEG, 95

BEGGED, 83
BELIEF, 86
BELIEVE, 78, 97-8, 101, 103
BELIEVED, 83-4
BIDDEN, 83
BOUND TO, 73-4

CALCULATE, 94
CALL (n.), 86
CALL (v.), 95
CALLED ON, 83
CAN, 28-42, 44, 48-50, 57n., 75-6, 79, 88n., 110, 118-19, 122-4, 126, 128-31, 135, 137, 141, 143-6, 150-1, 153, 155, 157
CAPABLE OF, 76
CAPACITY, 87, 126
CERTAIN, 10, 77-9
CERTAINLY, 89
CERTAINTY, 86
CLAIM (n.), 86
CLAIM (v.), 94, 96, 156
CLAIMED, 82-3
CLEAR, 81
CLEARLY, 89
COMMAND (n.), 86
COMMAND (v.), 95
COMMANDED, 83
COMMENT (n.), 86
COMMENT (v.), 94
COMMENTED, 82-3
COMPELLED, 84-5
COMPULSION, 86
COMPULSORY, 81-2
CONCEIVABLE, 85, 101
CONCEIVABLY, 89, 103
CONCLUDE, 94
CONJECTURE (n.), 86
CONJECTURE (v.), 94
CONJECTURED, 82-3
CONSIDERATION, 86
CONSIDERED, 83-4
CONSTRAINED, 83-4
CONVICTION, 86

* In most cases only the key word of the modal expression is given.

Subject Index

ability, 30-2, 36, 68, 76, 144
adjectival modal expressions, 3, 77-85, 101-4, 155-6
adjunction (of modal adverbs), 102-4
age (as variable in language acquisition), 140-4, 146-7
'A-indirectives', 17-18, 21
alethic modality, 4, 9-10, 14, 79-80, 89-90
ambiguity, 25-6, 47, 85; *see also under* polysemy
Amoy, 28
'andative' future, 71
aspect, 63-4, 70, 94, 134; *see also under* habitual aspect, progressive aspect *and* 'sporadic' aspect
assertions, 15-18, 24n., 44
assertive declarations, 23n.
assertives, 13-15, 23n., 24n.
attitudinal disjuncts, 89
autonomous syntax, 161

basic meaning—*see under* core meaning
Basque, 28
BE, 66-9
belief, 10, 23n.
'B-indirectives', 17, 21
boulomaic modality, 4, 9, 11, 14-15, 43-5, 76, 84, 87, 89, 97-8

categorical assertions, 15-18, 33, 67-8, 96
categorical directives, 15-18, 96
'category squish', 105
causal modality, 9, 11, 14
causation, 11, 43, 60
'centrality' (of modal auxiliary verbs), 100-5
'characteristic' (use of CAN), 31-2, 41
child language, 2-4, 28, 75-6, 107, 126-58, 160-2
circumstantial possibility, 144
Classical Aztec, 28
cognitive development, 2, 152-6, 162
commands, 15, 18, 37, 44
commissive directives, 23n.
commissives, 13-14

complementation, 66-8; *see also under* infinitival complements, gerundive complements *and* THAT-complements
'complex' modality, 31
complexity, 127, 152
comprehension, 129
conceptualist (approach to modality), 7-8, 47
conditionality, 50-6, 64
'conditionality' (use of WILL), 42, 46
conscious organization, 69-70
constatives, 12, 16, 24n.
constraints (on meaning of modal expressions), 35, 41, 48, 55, 160
context, 21-2, 26, 36
context of utterance, 16-17, 21, 39, 50-6, 65, 119-20, *and passim*
conventional implication, 43
conversational postulates, 24n.
cooperative commissives, 23n.
cooperative declarations, 23n.
Coptic, 67
core meaning, 3, 23, 25-9, 69, *and passim*
corpus-based (analysis of modal expressions), 4
cotext, 21, 63

decentering, 134, 155
declarations, 13-14
declarative sentence, 16
deixis, 108
deliberative questions, 113
demands, 15, 23n., 43
deontic modality, 4, 9, 11-12, 14-15, 18, 28, 34-9, 54-6, 58n., *and passim*
deontic source, 35, 41, 44, 55, 60-1, *and passim*
deontic statement, 24n.
derivational complexity hypothesis, 152
'derogatory' (sense of CAN), 32
descriptions, 13
desiderative function, 14-15
desideratives, 14
developmental psychology, 2, 127, 160-2
diachronic (analysis of modals), 34, 38, 41, 46-7